Those Sensational Soaps

Vilma Angel
Phil 4: 8 & 9

Those Sensational Soaps

VELMA ANGEL

UPLIFT BOOKS
Brea, California

Bible quotations are taken from the Amplified Bible, Old Testament, copyright ©1962, 1964 by Zondervan Publishing House, used by permission of Zondervan Bible Publishers; the Amplified New Testament, copyright ©The Lockman Foundation 1954, 1958; and The Living Bible, copyright©1971 by Tyndale House Publishers, used by permission.

The names of most persons mentioned in this book have been changed to protect their privacy.

Those Sensational Soaps

Copyright ©1983 by Velma Angel

Published by Uplift Books, 428 So. Brea Blvd., Suite B, Brea, CA 92621.

Library of Congress Cataloging in Publication Data

Angel, Velma.
  Those Sensational Soaps.

1. Soap operas – United States – History and criticism.
2. Soap operas – Religious aspects – Christianity.
I. Title.

PN1992.8.S4A53   1983   302.2'345   83-5818
ISBN 0-88005-003-9 (pbk.)

All rights reserved. This book may not be reproduced in any form without violation of copyright.

Printed in the United States of America

Acknowledgments

To those who have shared their time and knowledge with the subject of soap operas: Dr. Paul Risser, pastor of the Florence Avenue Foursquare Church; Dr. Margaret Stevens, pastor of the New Thought Church of Santa Anita; Rev. Darrell Roberts, associate pastor of the Church On The Way; Rev. Minnie Whaley, women's counselor, Church On The Way; Dr. Tom Snipes, Professor of Psychology, University of North Carolina, Boone, N.C.; Dr. Robert Merkel, psychologist and head of the counseling center of the Crystal Cathedral. To the pastors and group leaders who assisted in the surveys in their churches, and to the many women who were interviewed and gave their testimonies.

To the ABC, NBC, and CBS television networks for the information they supplied.

To Leona Adamo Clark, Diane Gilch and Karen Lee who edited and reviewed the manuscript.

Foreword

Foreword

Both in private counsel and public contact more and more leaders are discovering the destructive impact of "fantasizing." The spirit of fantasy is rampant today, and what may be innocent imaginations with a child, can become a crippling disease for an adult. 1 Corinthians 13:11 says, "When I became an adult, I put away childish things...." That statement comes from the greatest treatise ever written on *real* love.

Those Sensational Soaps explores a hideous invasion of the mind and its often devastating effects on the psychological well-being of the viewer. In a practical, personal and powerful manner, Velma Angel's book reveals a way of escape for those trapped by the lure of soap opera addiction. It will lead many away from the delusion and destruction of fantasies into the real world of happy fulfillment.

And that's the Creator's greatest gift to us all.

> Dr. Jack W. Hayford
> The Church On The Way
> Van Nuys, California

Introduction

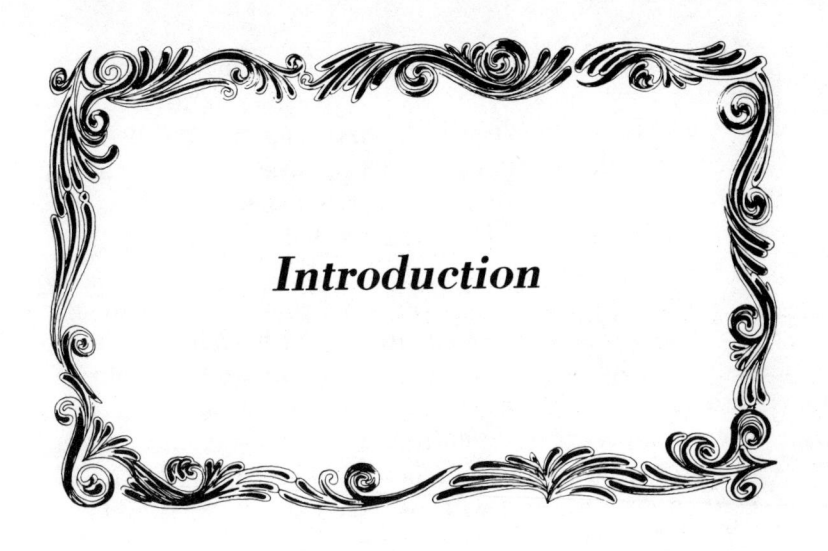

In just a few short years, the "Soaps" have gone from being the domain of the beleaguered housewife to enticing the interest of college students, the working public, and even professionals. Restaurants place television sets where their clientele can more readily catch the daily sagas during the lunch hour.

At the same time, the quality of soap programs is doubtful, because controls are virtually non-existent, and the content is produced with the belief that this is what the public wants. Therefore, the Christian who desires programming of a more significant quality finds it in short supply. Usually he ends up watching what is available rather than turning off the set.

Velma Angel, in *Those Sensational Soaps,* analyzes some of the dangers and problems she believes are occurring because of the influence of the "Soaps." In my opinion, the book reveals truth. Her research contains input from some of the best thinkers of the day, as well as Bible authors, writing under the inspiration of the Holy Spirit.

Most Christian writers have not singled out any particular part of television to investigate and write about. This work does just that! The "Soaps" have become such an important part of American life that they *must* be looked at with a critical eye. The Christian, above all, should evaluate all that he does in light of Godly principles.

Usually, we are careful about what we eat or drink because we know how food affects our health. But we seem less knowledgeable about the thoughts we put into our minds, forgetting that they eventually become a part of us and affect our emotional, spiritual and physical lives. Our intellectual diet is most significant in determining what we become as individuals and as Christians.

It is my hope that every concerned Christian will read this volume and seek to "burst the bubble" associated with watching the "soaps."

W. Thomas Snipes, Ed. D.
Professor of Psychology
Appalachian State University
Boone, North Carolina

Contents

Acknowledgments
v

Foreword
vii

Introduction
ix

Hooked on the Soaps
13

"Tune in Tomorrow for..."
31

Soaps Burst Into Big Business
49

Husbands, Wives and All Our Children
63

"Help Me! Dr. Katz"
73

Sensational or Sinsational?
89

Bursting the Soap Bubble
103

Hooked on the Soaps

1

At almost ten in the morning, Amelia was upset and irritable. Rushing to finish her household chores, she had knocked the box of crispy rice cereal onto the kitchen floor and muttered at her own stupidity and clumsiness. Hurriedly, she swept the food into the dustpan. Her mind raced . . . "only a few minutes left. Where has the morning gone!"

It had started like every other weekday – arising at seven as Michael left for work, waking Steven to get him ready for school, fixing him a breakfast of cold cereal and milk and pushing him out the door. Then baby Susan was fed and diapered. After stacking the dishes in the sink, Amelia picked up the newspapers scattered from the evening before and took out the trash. With one eye on the clock, she stuffed dirty clothes into the washing machine and set the dials. Finishing this chore at quarter to ten, she still had time to make fresh coffee and put Sue in her playpen with some toys.

Only a few minutes remained in her countdown

Those Sensational Soaps

when, reaching for her coffee cup, she'd sent the cereal box sailing. "Dummy!" she said to herself through clenched teeth. With three minutes to go, Amelia quickly poured herself a cup of coffee, rushed into the living room and switched on the television. Before the picture focused, the theme music of "Texas" filled the room. She breathed a sigh of relief, realizing she hadn't missed anything. Settling back on the sofa, she slowly sipped her coffee. Now her day could really begin.

Amelia watched intently as her favorite soap opera flashed on the screen, giving a reprise of the previous day's events. She'd been so worried about the situation with Gretchen, a character on the program, that she had had trouble sleeping during the night. Anxious to learn more of the absorbing drama, she eagerly focused all her attention on the unfolding action. Amelia's heart pounded as a terrified Gretchen shoved Ruby into a corner of the room. Her taunt fingers tightly clutched her coffee cup as her fictionalized friends encountered trauma after trauma. In her own living room, little Sue whined for a toy fallen out of the playpen. Without taking her eyes off the screen, Amelia bent down, retrieved the stuffed bear and tossed it back in. Gretchen had taken all the money, and as Ruby and Lurlene searched her apartment, they found an arsenal of weapons in the closet.

During the commercials, Amelia changed Sue, giving her cookies and new toys to keep her content and quiet. When the daily saga finally ended, she rushed to the kitchen with tears in her eyes to refill her coffee cup. Back in the living room, she switched the channel to "The Young and the Restless." In a highly emotional scene, Patty persuades Jack to drop the charges against Carl. But in return, Jack asks a favor, inviting her to his apartment and into his bedroom. After a toast, Jack tells Patty he desires her first sexual experience to be a special moment in her life. On the bed a scared Patty tightly clutches the covers, trying to hide her face from Jack. Absorbed completely, Amelia pulled the collar of her furry robe tightly around her throat as she watched. Jack begs Patty to show him the depth of her feelings, and in a rush of passion, they make love.

Abruptly, the story switched to Snapper, a character whom Amelia idolized. As the scene unfolded, Snapper was jeopardizing his marriage to Chris. Amelia shook her head in disbelief. "Not Snapper," she sobbed. Tears flooded her eyes as the musical theme ended the show.

Lunchtime was usually between "The Young and the Restless" and "General Hospital." But today with her throat tightened and stomach in knots, Amelia knew she would not be able to eat. Worry over the make-believe events she had just witnessed made eating unthinkable. Listlessly, she wandered into the kitchen to search the refrigerator for something to feed Sue. The potato salad from last week smelled funny, and she threw in into the garbage. A few slices of yellow cheese were left, but since the wrapping had come undone, it looked dried out and inedible. Suddenly, the problem of getting lunch seemed so overwhelming that she began to cry again. The baby, tired and hun-

Those Sensational Soaps

gry, joined her.

Frustrated, Amelia grabbed a bowl, filled it with what was left of the dry cereal and the last of the milk, and shoved it in front of the baby. Realizing that she was still in her bathrobe, she combed her hair and dressed. Pushing Sue in her stroller to the corner store, she methodically purchased a gallon of milk and a loaf of rye bread. On the way home, the bright noon sun bothered her eyes which were tight from crying. As she walked, her mind fastened on the problems seen in the morning soaps. "Oh, Snapper," she whined inwardly, "how could you be doing this?"

Susan was asleep by the time they reached home, so Amelia carried her softly into the house and up the stairs to her bedroom. She was careful not to wake her, knowing that she would sleep quietly through the afternoon soaps until Steven got home from school.

Amelia flopped down to watch "General Hospital" with a plate of toast and more black coffee. Once more she slipped back into her media world and picked up the threads of the story. Laura had been kidnapped, and Luke was distraughtly trying to find her. Just a few weeks before, Amelia remembered watching their beautiful wedding, crying tears of joy at their happiness. Now this had to happen. Laura had never had it easy, of course. So far, she'd been involved in a murder charge, rape, adultery and bootlegging. But with Luke by her side, Amelia reasoned, things would be different. During the commercials, Amelia stared at the olive green living-room carpet thinking, *Why, Lord, did You let that happen? It's not fair!*

Hooked on the Soaps

When Steven arrived home, Amelia, still worried and depressed, tried not to let her eight-year-old son see her red eyes. He must not know that she'd been crying. She quickly put both children out to play and began fixing dinner with a heavy heart.

Michael arrived home shortly before six, kissed her and asked if something were wrong. Amelia shrugged away and bit her lip, not replying. He just wouldn't understand. Watching her husband fall into a chair with the evening paper, she noticed his shirt buttons straining over his paunchy stomach. His hair needed trimming and his cheeks were dark with a six o'clock shadow. Amelia's thoughts returned to Snapper, so trim and dashing. She remembered Jack also, suave and well-dressed, sipping cocktails with Patty, paying her compliments. Momentarily, the greasy hamburgers frying on the stove faded into a vision of the elegant people she had spent her day with. That was the life she desired, and tomorrow at ten, she would live it again....

It is estimated that roughly forty percent of all homes with televisions are tuned in to at least one soap opera in a given week. Nielson figures indicate that soaps are the dominant force in daytime TV, attracting a larger audience than any other competing show.[1] As a Christian counselor, I have talked with hundreds of "Amelias" across the country—women suffering from this addiction, who display many recognizable symptoms. They exhibit depression, anxiety, apathy, a blurring of the distinction between reality and fantasy, and a feeling that they are not

Those Sensational Soaps

in control of their lives. Seeking counseling because of family or marital problems, they rarely recognize that the habitual, daily watching of soap operas has a negative effect on them.

A woman doesn't usually come for counseling saying, "I need help. I'm hooked on soap operas." But as she talks and thinks things through, she will often come to the conclusion that they are a contributing factor to her problems. As one woman put it, "Getting rid of the soaps was part of the healing that had to be done in my life."

Daily television soap operas attract an enormous, devoted audience, mainly female, which often identifies strongly with the soap characters. One extreme case of viewer identification through soap addiction was Harriet Green, who entered the Lace 'n Love Bridal Shoppe, her eyes brimming with joy and excitement.

"Something really elegant, maybe in a pale pink," she announced cheerfully to the sales clerk.

"Are you a relative or friend of the couple?" the clerk smiled, noting Mrs. Green's beaming enthusiasm. "Or the mother of the bride?"

"No, no," Mrs. Green assured. "I'm not a relative, but the couple is *very* special to me. You know, thousands of people are going to attend, and I feel absolutely delighted to be invited."

The saleswoman was taken aback by this, but then the thought hit her – *the royal wedding*? "It wouldn't be the wedding of Prince Charles and Lady Diana? How exciting!"

Mrs. Green scowled slightly, offended that the clerk

didn't know which wedding she was attending. "It's Luke and Laura's wedding," she announced grandly.
"Luke and Laura?"
"The couple on General Hospital!" Mrs. Green's frown deepened. "Luke is a doctor at the hospital, and they're getting married next week."
Mrs. Green was not an escapee from a mental institution. Nor was she drunk or senile. She was a perfectly respectable, forty-five-year-old matron, married, with three children, who cared for a lovely home and attended church regularly. Neither was Mrs. Green alone in her extreme involvement in Luke and Laura's wedding. Millions of viewers shed sentimental tears as the couple was joined in fake holy matrimony. From all over the country, Luke and Laura received wedding presents, congratulatory telegrams, cards, and letters wishing them well. More people watched their wedding than viewed the television of the real-life ceremony of Prince Charles and Lady Diana.

There is much evidence to indicate that many of the viewers are emotionally involved with the soap opera characters they watch. As Madeline Edmondson and David Rounds point out, "Much of the mail that producers receive speaks of the characters as real. Thousands and thousands of letters give advice, warn the heroine of impending doom, caution the innocent to beware..., inform one character of another's doings, or reprimand a character for unseemly behavior."[2] D.E. Tucker cited a report that television viewers sent approximately one-quarter of a million birthday cards

Those Sensational Soaps

when a character on "As the World Turns" turned sixty-five.[3]

The semblance of reality shown on the soaps is one of the keys to their tremendous appeal. Because the people on the programs seem real and their problems appear authentic, the viewer tends to identify with them. Yet the individuals and their problems are exaggerated and complicated, forcing simplistic solutions that can have powerful influence on the lives of habitual watchers. As Katzman has noted, "The almost-realism of the characters and themes, the repetition due to slow pace, and the extremely large number of hours spent viewing soap operas indicate that these shows have great potential power. They can establish or reinforce value systems. They can suggest how people should act in certain situations. They can legitimate behavior and remove taboos. . . ."[4]

Many troubled women are seeking help because of the turmoil in their lives. The experience of a woman I'll call Carol is typical of millions of others caught in this destructive trap. Here is her story as she told it:

> When I was a little girl, I did not lack attention. But because of the teaching and the pressure of being a "preacher's kid," I felt like I had a lot to live up to. I was always being judged on my performance. If it was not acceptable, then I was not accepted. This brought on distress, anxiety, fear, and guilt because I could never attain the perfection which was expected of me.
>
> When I was younger I read a lot and became involved with love stories. I then traded the books for

Hooked on the Soaps

the soaps.... I was not happy with my own self-image, and I determined to be whatever anyone wanted me to be. When I was with a certain group of people, I would act and be like I thought they wanted me to act and be. I always wanted to be accepted.

I was fourteen when I started watching the soaps, primarily because my mother did. I used to talk with my mom and friends about how terrible the soaps were, but it really did not seem to be a big thing. It was just something that everybody did.

I didn't notice any change in my life until I got married at the age of nineteen. Before I was married and living at home, we only watched a couple, but when I married I turned them on in the morning and watched them all day. My housework didn't get done, or if it did, it was between the story lines during the commercials.

I really didn't notice the hold they had on me. My parents were Christians, but there were so many hurts and lots of things that needed healing in my past. When I got married, I had to face some of the unhappiness of the past. The soaps became my scapegoat. I could live in the soaps, fantasize and never once have to worry about the real world. This happened when I was first entering into marriage, and I knew we should be building a relationship together. But on the soaps they fell in and out of love over and over again. They would be so happy in love until the next person came along.

I would build my time around the soaps. If I couldn't watch them, I became very agitated and upset. If for some reason I couldn't watch, as soon as I got home, I called a friend to see what had

Those Sensational Soaps

happened.

I went to sleep at night and if there had been something that had upset me about the soaps, or if I had not seen the outcome of the program, I dreamed the outcome of the story.... The forcefulness of the soaps so implanted the story in the subconscious that it became a part of my life. If something went wrong with one of the characters, I became very depressed. The soap was no longer a story; it was reality to me. I lived along with the drama. It became difficult for me to separate real life and fantasy. I related to them so strongly that I even absorbed some of the characteristics of the actors.

I had many physical problems during the time of the soap watching. How much was related to the programs I don't really know. I'm sure a great deal, as it kept me in such a state of anguish and depression. Getting rid of the soaps was a part of the healing that had to be done in my life. There were some emotional things that I would not have gotten rid of if I had continued to watch the programs.

Because the trauma that I had in my everyday life was fed by the soaps, they were a hindrance in my marriage. I don't think I had one favorite character, but instead I had several and would constantly compare my husband to them. I tried to force him to be like the soap characters. He didn't watch the soaps so he didn't even know what he was supposed to measure up to. I was dissatisfied with him. The soaps not only hurt my marriage, but they hindered my sexual relationship with my husband. My own husband became unattractive to me. I wanted him to be the ultimate in romance,... charming, good looking. I would pick out certain characteristics and tell him,

Hooked on the Soaps

"I wish you were like this," or "Why don't you do that?" It was a constant comparison. I watched the soaps all day, and when he came through the door there would be something wrong. I was always upset at something he did or didn't do.

During this time, I had a child. Often she was pushed aside as I didn't have time for her. I did not discipline her, and my main intention was to keep her quiet. Sometimes I knew I should have taken her for a walk, but I pushed a cookie in her hand instead. I don't think I really got angry with her, but I did anything and everything to keep her quiet. It wasn't until she was older that I began to feel completely guilty. I knew I wasn't doing things that needed to be done. At night I felt so bad because I had pushed her aside during the day. I neglected the child that was mine. The soaps did control my life.

I began to discover some real physical discomfort that definitely related to the program. I would have terrible headaches and, by the time my husband came home from work, my back would just be in knots. I was tense and uptight. Literally, I felt like someone had put clamps on me. One day I prayed, "Lord, something has to give. I can't stand living this way." I told the Lord I was just like a basket case and could not function as I needed to. I was desperate, so I prayed, "Lord, I'll do anything, anything Lord." In a small, still voice the Lord spoke to my spirit saying, "Will you give up 'Dark Shadows'?"

I tried to rationalize with the Lord, questioning Him as to "Why, Lord, why 'Dark Shadows'?" Again the Lord seemed to say, "Give it up for two weeks ...*two* weeks." I had been raised to listen to the voice of the Lord, so I gave it up. As soon as I did,

Those Sensational Soaps

the headaches and backaches went away. I never watched that program again. I watched some of the other soaps a little longer, and I began to see what a strong effect they had on me. Shortly after this, I stopped watching the soaps, seemingly one by one. I was so hooked on them, I don't know what gave me the ability to stop except God's grace. For some reason God had mercy on me and gave me extra strength to do what I had to do. It was hard. I had to unplug the TV, go outside and plan things away from home when the soaps were on.

Even today after several years of not watching the soaps I turn on the TV. As I'm turning the channel and a soap is on, I look at it and say, "Oh, that's interesting." I immediately turn the channel. The feeling that I have is almost like an alcoholic or one that has been on drugs. If I submit to that, I will be hooked again. I turn the channel and will not let myself get in the same bound situation as before.

Once the Lord frees you from something, you don't want to go back to it!

Obviously, Carol's self-esteem was critically low. Insecure about her own worth, she searched outside herself for answers to questions she should have found inward. Trying to escape her anxieties, she submerged herself in the daytime fantasies.

But with Carol, as with so many women, the image of life portrayed on the soaps was devastating. Women are always beautiful, dressed in the latest fashion, the ideal wife, lover and mother. Their homes are elegant and immaculate, and all their men are supreme lovers. The viewer who comes to believe that these people and

Hooked on the Soaps

places are real eventually compares this elegance to her own life.

The obvious differences cause greater anger, depression, and anxiety in women who are already angry, depressed and anxious. Their days are aimless and apathetic. Moral standards become confused and the ability to distinguish reality from fantasy blurs. Social interaction lessens as the soaps demand a large amount of time which stiffles communication with family and friends. Fatigue due to stress and a lack of physical activity is a constant complaint. Yet, as a woman's emotional and social problems mount, she looks more and more to the soaps for an escape, thus producing the vicious circle.

But the viewers aren't the only ones who strongly identify with the soap characters. Virginia Dwyer, who became Mary Matthews on "Another World" for several years, related her own involvement. Going through her clothes closet one bright sunny afternoon, she was startled by the realization that every article there was the style and color that "Mary Matthews" would have worn, and nothing like what she herself would have chosen. She panicked and threw all the clothes out, realizing that in a very real sense she had *become* Mary Matthews.[5]

Val Dufour, an actor who plays John Wyatt on "Search for Tomorrow," has reported a similar experience. The character John Wyatt always wears expensive suits and shirts, flashy diamond rings, with lots of wrist and neck chains. Dufour says, "I've never dressed that way in my life. But now that I'm doing it on the show, I suddenly find myself buying fancy suits, tight shirt collars, and the same sort of jewelry. I stroll through Bloomingdale's looking at John Wyatt-type clothing, and I ask myself, 'Why am I doing this?' "[6]

One soap actress who is careful about what she does and why is Elvera Roussel, who plays the part of Hope Bauer on "The Guiding Light." She has made the following statement:

> I'm not setting myself up as Miss Morality or whatever, for in my private life, I'm not perfect. On the screen, however, when I'm playing a role model, I think she should be human, have her frailties and her faults, but the character must be responsible to the audience. I will not be stuck with what will influence an audience in a bad way. The responsibility should be in each of us. We are in a medium that influences people unbelievably. They are doing studies on soap operas now and the influence that we have, and we do have mass influence. I go into producers every day and discuss issues if I don't feel it's right for the character.[7]

The part of Hope Bauer, she believes, is more than just a role. Hope is usually portrayed as a good and loving mother, a family person who stands behind her husband (although he is far from ideal) and works hard at her career. Because of all these attributes, Elvera realizes that a lot of people look up to Hope as a role model. This makes it extremely important that her actions in the soap are consistent.

The responsibility Elvera feels toward her audience is particularly strong when it comes to the children who watch. "I get a lot of mail from every age group," she says, "but I get a great deal of mail from young kids, and I have a responsibility to those children."[8]

Elvera is passionately outspoken about an actor's moral obligation and has chosen the roles she plays accordingly. "Too often people go around doing things without thinking, and I am so tired of hearing actors say, 'Well, I was paid to play the role... I'm just acting out a part.' You are responsible for the role you play. There is nothing in the book that says you have to go out and play a pimp and make him look good."[9]

There is no doubt that the soap opera craze is having a vast influence on the American economy, as well as the family. What started almost by accident in the early days of radio has become television's multi-million dollar stepchild. Does it offer harmless entertainment — an innocent escape from mundane problems? Or is it a hideous trap from which millions need release? To find the answer, I delved deeply into soap opera roots, intent on analyzing the "Tune in Tomorrow..." complex.

2

"Tune in Tomorrow for..."

2

Bill: *I love you, Rosemary, the way a man loves life — the way he feels when he's on the battlefield and men are dead all around him, and he's unhurt and takes great gulps of air into his lungs and sobs, "I'm alive!" — that's how I love you....*

Rosemary: *Oh, Bill....*

Bill: *I love you the way a man loves — loves his home, and the sky at night full of stars, and a fire on the hearth — the way he loves the ocean, and the way he loves mountains, and the way he loves little quiet places under the trees....*

Rosemary: *Bill!...Bill!*

Bill: *My darling...my love...my precious (sound of kisses)....*[1]

Those in charge of programming in the infant days of radio — the 1920s — knew they had a vast, untapped market in the housewives of America. If they could provide entertainment that women could

Those Sensational Soaps

enjoy while they scrubbed the family's laundry on the washboard, kneaded bread, beat the carpets, and waxed the furniture, they would capture the housewives' attention and pocketbooks. They reasoned that even the screechy sounds and waves of static that plagued early radio would be music to the ears of the lonely housewife as she toiled over her monotonous daily chores. But what sort of program would have the most appeal?

Evening programs such as music, news, political speeches, prize fights and sermons had already been tried. And, they were largely unsuccessful in the daytime. Then, quite accidentally, an announcer in Chicago, Norman Brokenshire, hit upon a program format that filled the bill.

He had a half-hour of air time each day during which he presented what could be called a variety show. It was mostly garden-type variety, but he did have one interesting innovation. He featured vaudeville acts which were appearing in the area. The vaudevillians benefitted by publicizing their act, and Brokenshire succeeded in adding a bit of professional sparkle to his program.

Brokenshire was especially pleased one day with the vaudevillians he had booked for his show. Everything was set, and he had the entertainers' enthusiastic commitment, or so he thought. They were going to fill his half-four program with topnotch acts. But as air time approached, Brokenshire became painfully aware that signals had somehow gotten crossed. The performers simply hadn't shown up. Still, the show, as he well knew, had to go on. When his cue came from the sound room, he began to ad-lib. Suddenly, his eyes fell on a book lying within reach and, in desperation, he grabbed it and began to read. He put everything he had into the story — every inflection, dramatic pause, every bit of excitement he could muster — in an effort to somehow entertain the audience.

Eventually, the prearranged performers arrived and got Brokenshire off the hook. But during the next few days, to everyone's amazement, the station was deluged with letters of applause. The audience had loved Brokenshire's dramatic reading! Their only complaint was that he hadn't finished the story. What, they demanded, happened next?

It became obvious to Brokenshire and to the station's executives that they had inadvertantly stumbled on just the kind of program the daytime listening audience wanted — serialized drama. It was the beginning of a new era for the still infant radio.[2]

"The Smith Family" aired in 1925, following quickly after Brokenshire's fortunate ad-libbing. It was known as a continuing "domestic drama," although it did in fact feature a great deal of comedy. It was the story of a mother and her two daughters. The daughters — of marrying age — were being courted by two young men, one a prize fighter and the other Jewish. The audience loved the "complications" that followed, filled with dramatic twists and comic situations. The series was presented once a week, with the same characters appearing regularly. So it was essen-

Those Sensational Soaps

tially the type of drama that came to be known as a soap opera, although it did have a bit more humor than the later programs.[3]

Within a year after "The Smith Family," the fabulously successful "Amos 'n Andy Show" was created by Charles Correll and Freeman Gosden. In their search for an innovative plot that would capture a listening audience, they hit upon the idea of a comedy based on Negro life. The story line revolved around two young fellows from a small town in Alabama who were seeking their fame and fortune in a big city. These characters were a study in contrasts: Andy was pleasant, willing to work, easily made friends and was ready to cooperate in all sorts of circumstances. Amos was the direct opposite—lazy, fast-talking, and ready to con anyone out of anything.

Correll and Gosden not only wrote the scripts but also acted the parts. They were not Negro, but their accents were authentically Deep South, so convincing that most listeners would never have believed that they were listening to white actors.

The writing and acting team desired to expand their Chicago-based show to a nationwide audience, but in order to do that they needed two basics—air time and a sponsor. Pepsodent, a brand of toothpaste, was willing to back them. But air time, the type they were looking for, was more difficult to come by. Up until that time the NBC network was broadcasting only half-hour and hour shows. But Correll and Gosden wanted to negotiate a contract for fifteen minutes of air time six days a week. The opposition was stiff, but the team was persistent. After persuading the network that a continuous story line could be presented six days a week successfully, Correll and Gosden began airing "Amos 'n Andy" across the country on NBC in 1929.[4]

The authors proved to be right. "Amos 'n Andy" became the rage with the American listening public. In the peak years of the show, it is believed that fifty percent of American families who owned radios listened to the program regularly. Telephone companies noticed that their business slackened considerably during the broadcast. Even if you were out for an evening stroll during that particular fifteen minute period, you would not necessarily miss the program. Through open windows you were sure to catch the episode, because home after home would have the number one program in the nation blaring loudly.

Although basically a comedy, "Amos 'n Andy" also had a touch of drama and, occasionally, sadness. It was a program that most people could enjoy and relate to. The problems were everyday, human dilemmas solved with humor and common sense. Of course, many of the comic situations were based on racial stereotypes that today would be offensive.

In the excerpt from the show which follows, Amos and Andy are preparing to take a trip to Chicago. Money is a problem, so they are trying to figure out how much their tickets will cost:

Amos: *Come on—let's sit down yere an' figger dis thing out.*

Those Sensational Soaps

Andy: *Now lissen yere — $26.72 — dat's whut it cost each one of us.*

Amos: *Now you is got to times dat by two, ain't you?*

Andy: *Wait till I do dat yere — twenty-six, seventy-two — times two. Two times two is — a —*

Amos: *Dat's four.*

Andy: *No, no — two an' two is four. We is timesin' yere now.*

Amos: *Well, two times two is four, ain't it?*

Andy: *Whut we is got do is to mulsify. You is stackin' em up, dat's whut you is doin'. Two times two — wait a minute yere now — two times two is six.*

Amos: *Two times two is six, huh?*

Andy: *An' Nothin' to carry — now — a — two times seven — dere's one right dere. We is two timesin' $26.72 — two times two is six — nothin' to carry — two times seven.*

Amos: *Dat's two sevens, ain't it?*

Andy: *Dat can't be seventeen, kin it?*

Amos: *I know whut dat is. Wait a minute yere — lemme count it on my fingers yere. Dat's fo'teen, ain't it?*

Andy: *Dat's whut I jest said. Put down a fo' an'*

"Tune in Tomorrow for . . ."

	carries one. Now, I'll put dat one up yere by dat six two times sixteen —
Amos:	*Whut you goin' do now — mulsify sixteen, huh?*
Andy:	*Well, I got carry dat one — I puts dat one right in between dat two an' de six.*
Amos:	*Whut is we mulsifyin'?*
Andy:	*We'se mulsifyin' $26.72 by two. You see, de fust thing is two times two is six — two times seven is fo'teen — an' I carries one — so dat goes right in between de two an' de six.*
Amos:	*Dat goes right in between de two an' de six, don't it? Put it dere now an' lemme see how it looks.*
Andy:	*Wait a minute yere now — I'll put de one in between de two an' de six — dat makes 216 now.*
Amos:	*Is you goin' mulsify dat 216?*
Andy:	*Course I goin' mulsify — whut you think I goin' do wid it.*
Amos:	*Well, whut is dat 216 — is dat 216 dollars?*
Andy:	*You see where I done put dat dot in dere, don't you? Dat makes dat $216.*
Amos:	*Well, when did we get up in dem big figures?*

Those Sensational Soaps

Andy: *Dat's whut happened when you mulsify.*

Amos: *Well, go ahead, do it. You know whut you is doin' dere.*

Andy: *Two times 216 — lemme see — how much is $216 times two?*

Amos: *Well, figgerin' it out in my own haid yere, I figures dat dat's over $400.*

Andy: *I b'lieve you is right — Dat is right — dat's over $400. Two times $26.72, de way I figures yere, is over $400.*

Amos: *Dat certainly is a lot o' money fur us to git up dere on, ain't it?*

Andy: *Lissen — I got a idea — we'll fool 'em. I'll go one day an' give $26.72 — den de nex' day don' say nothin' to em an' you give $26.72 an' we'll both git dere.*

Amos: *Dat's a idea — boy, you certainly do think of 'em.*[5]

"Amos 'n Andy" was certainly a different kind of situation comedy. The story line would make you laugh, but the characters inspired empathy and affection in the listeners, too. The show became a huge national success. The sponsor, Pepsodent toothpaste, also benefited because they were selling more toothpaste than ever before. Other programs followed: "Lum and Abner," "Moonshine and Honeysuckle," "Clara, Lu 'n Em," "Vic and Sade." The radio audience

"Tune in Tomorrow for..."

was growing, and they liked what they were beginning to hear.

"The Goldbergs," another extremely popular soap, originated about this time. Like "Amos 'n Andy," it also portrayed people of an ethnic background with rather stereotyped humor. But despite this, the Goldbergs were human, likeable characters and the program had a long and successful run from 1929 to 1945 on NBC.[6]

In addition to popular programs, radio also produced its share of famous writers. Names like Irna Phillips, Elaine Carrington, and Frank and Anne Hummert will be remembered for their contributions to the history of soap operas.

Miss Phillips was the creator and writer of such well-known soaps as "Painted Dreams," "Woman in White," "Right to Happiness," "The Guiding Light," "Road of Life," and "Lonely Woman." A bright, energetic woman, Irna reached a turning point in her life at age 28. She had a teaching job in a children's theater, but was dissatisfied with it.

While in Chicago, she visited the radio broadcasting studios there. The director mistakenly assumed that she had come to try out for a part and gave her a script to read. She read it with ease and enthusiasm. She was offered a position immediately, but refused it when she learned that it did not include a salary! Although she had a talent for telling stories, she would not and could not work for free.

She returned home. But not long after, she relented, returned to Chicago, and accepted the unpaid posi-

Those Sensational Soaps

tion. After a period of time at the Chicago-based station, WGN, she was offered a salary of $50 a week to write a "family serial." Eventually called "Painted Dreams," the serial had a story line which revolved around a mother, her grown children and their friends. The theme was that love, marriage, and motherhood were a woman's ultimate fulfillment and should be her highest dream.

Miss Phillips became an overnight success. Her writing was powerful, and her creative storytelling captured the attention and the hearts of the audience. A prolific writer, she was known to turn out as much as 60,000 words of script a week. She dictated her scripts to a secretary, either pacing back and forth and acting out all the parts of the soap, or else perching on the arm of a chair while she spun her story. Her work paid well. By the mid-1930s, she was making about a quarter of a million dollars a year. For forty years she churned out some of the most successful soaps on radio, and her influence continued to be felt when soaps made the move to television.[7]

The daily dramas of the 1930s contained much sentimentality and romanticism, but very little action. Attempting to play on what the writers considered the "feminine" nature of their audiences, the plots included lots of tears and fluffy emotionalism. This seemed to be a successful formula for another of the famous writers of the early soaps—Elaine Carrington. The typically romantic, florid scene that begins this chapter is one of hers, from the very popular soap, "Rosemary."

Carrington, according to soap opera lore, dictated her scripts from 10 o'clock to 4 o'clock every working day, with only a short break for lunch. Sometimes dictating scenes while lounging across a seven-foot bed, she was able to write three different shows at one time, and apparently did it well. Although most radio script writers were anonymous, she was unusually well known since her name was prominently mentioned before and after each of her shows. The announcer might say, "Procter and Gamble White Laundry Soap—for cleaner, whiter clothes—brings you 'Rosemary'!" After a dramatic pause he would continue, "'Rosemary,' written by Elaine Carrington, author of 'Pepper Young's Family' and 'When a Girl Marries,' is dedicated to all young women of today." And so Elaine Carrington's name became a household word.[8]

Two other soap opera writers, the team of Frank and Anne Hummert, have been given much credit for originating the idea of the soap opera. They were responsible for many of the popular serialized stories of the 1930s and 1940s, including, "Amanda of Honeymoon Hill," "Backstage Wife," "David Harum," "Front Page Farrell," "John's Other Wife," "Just Plain Bill," "Lorenzo Jones," "Nona from Nowhere," "Our Gal Sunday," "The Romance of Helen Trent," "Stella Dallas," "Young Widder Brown," and "Bob and Betty."[9]

A key to the Hummerts' success was their idea that soap stories should be about the everyday activities of ordinary people, and that they should be written so that listeners could relate to them whether they

Those Sensational Soaps

lived in a Fifth Avenue penthouse or in an adobe hut on the desert. In addition, Frank Hummert believed that a good story deserved expert promotion. He was not only a talented writer, but had an instinct for business and advertising, which eventually paid off. By 1938 their radio time was worth $12 million a year, and they had written more than six and a half million words.[10]

Because audiences loved the soaps, legions of writers, editors, and script readers worked hard to mass produce them, not realizing perhaps the pervasive influence their content would have on America.

Today, the backgrounds, attitudes and views of soap writers and editors are still projected in the dramas. Research indicates that soap writers are predominantly highly educated white males in their 30s and 40s. They are ideologically liberal and strongly support environmental protection, affirmative action, women's rights, homosexual privileges and sexual freedom. Their cosmopolitan, liberal point of view often differs from "mainstream America."

On various moral issues, their attitudes contrasted sharply from those of the public. Fifty-four percent of the media staff people did not regard adultery as wrong, and only fifteen percent saw extra-marital affairs as immoral. Ninety percent of them supported women's right to abortion and seventy-five percent did not think homosexuality improper. In comparison, eighty-five percent of the public viewed adultery as sinful, sixty-five percent considered abortion morally indecent, and seventy-one percent believed homosexuality was wrong.

Only eight percent of those interviewed went to church or synagogue weekly, compared with forty-one percent of the public. Eighty-six percent seldom or never attended religious services, and fifty percent disclaimed any religious affiliations. In contrast, seventy percent of the public possessed some religious tie.

Of course, even as today, early soap writers emphasized and often exaggerated the headaches and heartaches of everyday life. But this added drama to the continuing story, and spectacle was what the audience wanted. With some subtle differences, they told the story of everyday American life with which listeners could identify. For example, almost everyone on the soaps had a white-collar job or profession. Blue-collar laborers were rare. The people portrayed were, for the most part, middle class. Occasionally, characters were wealthy or of ethnic backgrounds, perhaps Italian or Jewish.

Work in soapland had little relationship to the labor done in real life, because the jobs the characters held provided them with unlimited free time. Their work situations were merely occasions for them to meet and interact with the other characters: no real *work* was actually done. The doctor had plenty of time for romance in the afternoon. The businessman's office was always open to a parade of friends with problems to share. No scheduled appointments cramped his style! And the woman of the house never had to wash dishes, clean bathrooms, or dust furniture. Of course,

Those Sensational Soaps

an element of fantasy for the listening housewife was in all of this: what homemaker wouldn't trade her broom, mop, and frying pan for a world in which she had plenty of time to do just what she'd like?

But all this free time was absolutely necessary to the characters on the soaps. Because without it, how could they possibly fall in love again and again? And on the soaps, almost everyone fell in love over and over. Romance was the stuff soaps were made of, and romance takes time.

Divorces, deaths and remarriages filled the screen hour by hour. The complicated romances led to the birth of many babies of unknown parentage – often fathered by someone other than the mother's current husband. But these babies were quite accommodating, disappearing regularly after a few episodes. This eliminated the drudgery of actual childrearing and freed the parents to continue their romances. Occasionally, the children would be written into the story again when full-grown and likely candidates for their own romances.

Certainly, this continued unreality presented a distorted view of family life. Few good marriages or happy families were shown. Characters in the soaps were usually one-dimensional and had no interest in hobbies, politics, education or self-improvement. No one was dedicated to a cause, and religion was unimportant. Examples of goodness and kindness to one's fellowman were occasionally demonstrated, but truly religious characters were never portrayed. A priest may have presided over a wedding or a funeral, and a

"Tune in Tomorrow for..."

Christmas story may have been read to a child, but that was the extent of religion.

Pine Valley, Lonesome Hollow, Simpsonville, and Springdale were the small country towns which the audience could imagine as quiet, peaceful and serene. Yet they were places where everyone's problems, joys and sorrows were common knowledge. And the listening public loved and tuned into this semblance of reality. When the soaps made their transition to television in 1951 with the program "Search for Tomorrow," more than seven and a half million women between the ages of 18 and 49 followed. Soapland could now be watched as well as heard; it could be seen rather than imagined.

3

Soaps Burst Into Big Business

3

If the soaps on radio were romantic, rose-colored, and perhaps even ridiculous, the soaps on television have become tantalizing, tempting, and torrid. In the 1980s more than thirty million viewers can watch "General Hospital," "All My Children," "One Life to Live," and "The Young and the Restless." The story lines are, as TV critic Charles Sopkin describes them, confusing and amazing. Sex has become more explicit, making the soap operas even more popular.

A typical afternoon in TV soapland finds the viewer ingrossed in the problems of Mr. Cortlandt on "All My Children." He has divorced his first wife, Daisy, threatened her life, and is now married to the young and beautiful Donna. Donna wants a family and becomes pregnant. Is the child Mr. Cortlandt's or Chuck's, Donna's first husband? Since the rich but elderly Mr. Cortlandt is not interested in having any more children, he gives an out-of-town doctor a large sum of money so that Donna can abort the child. Will Donna carry the child to term? Are her prelabor pains

Those Sensational Soaps

a symptom of her anxiety that will cause her to lose the baby?

In the next scene, Mr. Cortlandt and Daisy, his first wife, sip champagne and eat caviar in a plush hotel suite in New York. They have slipped away to the city to mend the differences they've had in the past, and, of course, to make love. They laugh and giggle like two teenagers on their first date. Is Mr. Cortlandt trying to win his first wife back and get rid of Donna who is having the baby? Tune in tomorrow for more romance at high noon.

The next soap opens symbolically – the orchestra playing background music while birds fly through white snowy clouds in a blue sky. Suddenly, the clouds darken as though a storm is brewing. A ray of light pierces them and grows steadily brighter. Across the middle of the screen flashes a beautiful rainbow, as once again white clouds form the background for the words, "One Life to Live." Then follows the parade of commercials: an orange drink to satisfy some thirsty but adorable children; a brand of coffee to score a victory for a wife when her husband asks for a second cup, a lotion to soften and scent a naked baby; a truckload of lemons to supply a household that has switched to a lemony dish detergent.

After three minutes of advertisements, the soap begins. Pat and Tony sit on a couch, discussing wedding plans, embracing often. Should it be a large wedding or a small one? Saint Luke's Chapel, of course. How about the honeymoon? Will Pat take time off from work? She hesitates, then agrees. More commer-

Soaps Burst Into Big Business

cials interrupt for sugarless chewing gum, canned ravioli, allergy capsules and instant mashed potatoes. As we return to the characters' lives, a busybody named Adrian—every soap has at least one—pays a visit. Tony rejoins Pat, revealing that his job as a movie stuntman has been rescheduled, and he won't be able to make it to the honeymoon. Pat is upset because she has already rearranged her work schedule. Is the wedding still on? Tune in tomorrow.

And so it goes—hour after hour of romantic crises, with fifteen minutes of each hour devoted to selling soap, food and pills. And that, of course, is what soaps are all about, from the station's point of view—selling.

Soaps even got their name from the products first sold by the radio advertisers on the dramatic serials. The makers of soap and cleaning products saw those shows as the perfect way to reach the housewife. If they could get her ear and convince her that their product would clean better, be easier on the hands, add a lovely fragrance to her laundry, or save her money, they'd sell more soap. Today that marketing theory has spread to the whole range of products women buy—not just soap, but food, fashions, and pharmaceuticals. Women spend America's money, and they can be reached through soaps.

In the past few years, the daily dramas have become so popular that all sorts of products have spun off from them. At least nineteen newsstand magazines and publications are devoted to the daytime soaps and the personalities who are the stars. Key rings, bumper stickers, and T-shirts have appeared

Those Sensational Soaps

related to the programs. Soap fans can even get together to play the new "General Hospital Game," which retails for $9.99. The object of the game is to block or doublecross your friends, blackmail your enemies, and see how many romances you can have with the different characters. While playing the "General Hospital Game" you can sip coffee from a mug that proclaims the name of your favorite soap or perhaps just makes the blanket statement—"I love the soaps." Your cigarettes can be snuffed out in soap opera ashtrays, your walls can be decorated with soap opera posters, and your lapels can sport soap opera buttons.

And if you're really a fan, you can purchase some soap opera real estate. The Southfork Ranch—made famous by the infamous J. R. Ewing and his clan on "Dallas"—has become the center of tourism and trade in the Dallas-Fort Worth area, as the following story published in the Dallas Times Herald indicates:

> For almost four years, visitors by the thousands have flocked here from around the world to get a glimpse, a photograph—and sometimes a piece—of the ranch made famous by the television series "Dallas."
>
> In self-defense, hundreds of gas station attendants, convenience store clerks and hotel bellhops in a 50-mile radius have memorized or even mimeographed directions to the home of the fictional First Family of Oil.
>
> The Southfork mystique has created rural traffic

Soaps Burst Into Big Business

jams, destroyed privacy and once caused neighbors to sue in an unsuccessful attempt to halt filming at this southern Collin County ranch. But nearby homeowners have learned to cope.

So, too, have the ranch's owners, Joseph R. "J. R." Duncan, his wife, Natalie, and their three sons.

They used to padlock the iron gate down by the road and hide from the gawkers, but these days they welcome them with open arms – and pen palms. Those tourists have made Southfork the Dallas-Fort Worth area's No. 1 tourist attraction.

And they've transformed the reluctant Duncans into savvy salesmen, proud of the ranch that leads No. 2 Neiman-Marcus and the now-third-ranked Kennedy assassination site in the ability of Dallas attractions to draw a crowd.

"We had elected not to do this sort of thing," said Duncan, gesturing toward his souvenir stand and the tourists brazenly inspecting every inch of his pool. 'But they waved enough money at us that I yielded, and, well, one thing led to another."

The old "No Admittance" sign that used to hang over the gate is long gone. Thanks to Duncan and a few other area entrepreneurs, the one-time family farm has been transformed into a peddler's paradise, offering a basic lesson in ranch retailing.

Now, on most days, the gates are swung open and visitors are welcome to take a free walk about 500 feet up the driveway where Duncan's trailer vending stand sits, offering wares including Southfork T-shirts, strips of postcards (the only way to see the house's interior), gold or brass belt buckles (the most expensive is $50) and plastic candy dishes – in two sizes – embossed with a color photo of the ranch.

Those Sensational Soaps

For those who long for a piece of the ranch, there are clear plastic paperweights enshrouding a bit of "Southfork dirt" ($13), novelty deeds for one-square-inch pieces of the property ($4), or real deeds for a square foot of Southfork Ranch ($20). Both documents are emblazoned, of course, with a photo of the "Other" J. R. – Ewing, that is.

Then there are black and white bumper stickers, key rings and baseball caps with the ranch's brand, and even a Southfork cookbook.

To go any farther down the expansive, black driveway toward the white-columned house and the equally famous pool, costs $4 – even for babes in arms.

Therein lies a bit of Southfork trivia. The reason visitors can get a whole 500 feet onto the property for free is because the front portion of the land lies in the city of Parker, where no retail sales of any kind are allowed. Fortunately for Duncan, the rest of the 164-acre ranch sprawls outside the Parker corporate limits.

There's no way to know how many thousands of visitors have walked up the drive or posed for pictures by the famous gateway, Duncan said.

Things have changed at the spread that used to be called "Duncan Farms."

The turning point came when a curious tourist offered one of Duncan's sons a $100 bill to see the property.

Then the souvenir trailers went up, and by mid-1980, Duncan had set aside four acres of the property to be sold by the foot and the inch.

So far, about 1,100 people from all over the world

Soaps Burst Into Big Business

have registered the deeds to their one-foot parcels with the Collin County clerk. Although Duncan won't say how many he has sold, he did say about 12,000 of the square-inch parcels have been snapped up. At the square-inch rate, he will get about $25 million an acre, while at the square-foot rate, it comes to a mere $871,200 per acre.

Even native Texans have shown their love for the show and the ranch, Duncan said, explaining that they have paid as much as $650 for a square-foot deed and $500 for a 24-carat gold-plated belt buckle in charity auctions.

Duncan, 48, a tall, stocky Texan who covers his salt-and-pepper hair with a Southfork baseball cap, is nearly as apologetic about his new-found source of income as the visitors are about their fascination with the ranch.

He loves it.

He's changed the 12-year-old ranch's legal name to Southfork. "After all," he pointed out, "we are south of the fork" of Parker Road and Farm-to-Market Road 2551 just northeast of Plano.

He's succumbed to many of the hundreds of requests to rent the ranch for parties and weddings, and last winter built a 500-person "party barn" so he could host events all year long. He wouldn't say how much a Southfork party costs but promised, "If they've got the budget, we can accommodate them and leave them with happy memories."

When actor Jim Davis, who played family patriarch Jock Ewing, died last year, the Duncans bought Jock's blue Lincoln Continental just to park in the driveway for the tourists to see.

Those Sensational Soaps

So far, two sets of "EWING 1" license plates have been stolen off the car, but Duncan has a third set on order.

The tourists who took them "probably don't think they're stealing; they just want souvenirs," Duncan said, adding with a laugh that he doesn't know "how in the world they got them off" without being seen.

But he said he does watch his guests, if for no other reason than to get an idea of how well the show is doing and where. He said he can tell what new country the television series is playing in by the nationality of his guests.

After the show began playing in West Germany and Japan last summer, he said, busloads of tour groups from those countries parked out on the two-lane road that runs by the ranch.

"You're never going to believe this," Duncan said, "but one man really convinced me that he had come all the way from Frankfurt, (West) Germany, just to see this place."

With each new country into which Lorimar sends the show, Duncan has a new potential market. Many of his souvenirs are selling in England, Ireland, Scotland, South Africa, West Germany and Australia.

But not every aspect of Duncan's business interests are tied to the tourists. He has raised two world champions from his herd of about 30 quarter horses at the ranch.

And he has diversified his interests in other ways. After phasing out his land-development company last year, he took a cue from the show's fictional Ewing clan and formed the Southfork Exploration Co. Ltd. to search for oil. "We might be drilling the 'Sue

Soaps Burst Into Big Business

Ellen 1' soon," he joked, referring to J. R. Ewing's former wife.

Duncan said Southfork's future could include some location shots for cable TV shows and perhaps more commercials, like the one filmed recently featuring Cowboy defensive tackle Randy White.

For however long it lasts, the seven-day-a-week tourist business will be welcome, Duncan said, simply because "It's worth it."

It can take a toll, he admits, but even the constant invasions of privacy have their merits.

"I didn't think I'd ever be glad to see a peeping Tom," Duncan said, "but at four bucks a pop, they can peek all they want."

CBS originally selected the Duncan ranch for the series because of its physical look and isolated location. The cast of "Dallas" spends about two months each year on location there.[1]

Yes, television soap operas have become big business. In sheer numbers, their following is enormous with estimates ranging from twenty million viewers to as many as sixty million. One of the reasons spin-off businesses related to the dramas are so successful is that to many viewers the programs are much more than TV fantasy. They consider the soaps real. And for many, they are an addiction.

4

Husbands, Wives and All Our Children

4

Although the overwhelming majority of habitual soap opera viewers are women, men are not immune to the lure of soap opera addiction. Jonathan, for example, became addicted to the soaps as a small boy. In the late 1930s, when the Depression began to ease a little, his mother and father scraped up enough money to buy the family a radio. Soon after that, he suffered a seige of the measles and had to stay home from school.

To keep Jonathan quiet, his mother let him listen to the radio while she went about her housework. Switching the dial from station to station, he discovered radio soap operas. Something about the stories fascinated him, and for the two weeks that he lay in bed recuperating, he listened to every program he could. They became an obsession with him.

After he returned to school, Jonathan could not concentrate on the math problems the teacher was posing or on the spelling test he was taking; his mind was on the soap operas. He lost interest in school and

Those Sensational Soaps

began faking headaches, stomach aches, sore throats, coughs – anything that would allow him to stay home and listen to the soaps. While in high school, Jonathan had to be disciplined by his parents because of his lack of interest and failing grades. He was forbidden to listen to the soaps for two years. During that time, he suffered stomach disturbances and attacks of nervousness and depression because he was sitting in a classroom while his favorite programs were on the air.

When he went to college, soaps were making the transition to TV. Only the very wealthy boys had small TVs in their rooms, and Jonathan worked his way into their company just to have the opportunity to watch the soaps.

Long out of college, Jonathan still watches the soaps, and "All My Children" is his favorite. He is pleased that the dramas receive such high ratings and that they are an important part of our society. "Soaps are such a part of my life," he admits, "that if I had to stop watching them now, I would have a complete nervous breakdown."

The negative effects which soap operas have on the habitual viewer's self-image and value system are multiplied when that person is a child. Yet mothers who watch soaps often allow their children to do so also. And many children – teenagers and younger – are addicted.

Jim was a boy of twelve who attended a Christian school. He was studious and liked sports. Chemistry was his favorite subject, and he delighted in handling lizards and creepy bugs – especially when he

Husbands, Wives and All Our Children

could tease the girls with them. In other words, he was a normal boy.

One day Jim was caught stealing an item from his teacher's desk. There was little theft in the school Jim attended, because the students were taught integrity, decency and good behavior. They were loved, cared for, and disciplined. Therefore, Jim's teacher was puzzled by his behavior.

When questioned, Jim explained himself this way: "I know I did wrong, but I didn't think I'd get caught. When my dad is speeding and sees a cop coming up behind him, he says, 'Oh, oh, I gotta slow down. The cop's after me. I'll turn off this street and maybe he won't notice.' He doesn't get caught.

"And when I get home from school," he continued, "I watch the soap stories with my mom. Sometimes it's kinda dumb, all the kissing and stuff, but the other afternoon it was good. A guy on the soap killed his business partner, and he didn't even have to go to jail!"

Obviously Jim was using the input he was getting from his family and from the soap operas to establish his value system. And he is far from being alone. According to recent research, many, many children across the country are watching the soap operas daily. The following comments are typical responses which we received in our survey:

"I am ten years old. I like 'General Hospital'."

"I am thirteen years old and my favorite soap operas are 'The Young and the Restless,' 'Days of Our

Those Sensational Soaps

Lives,' and 'Another World'."

"I am fourteen years old, and I'm crazy about Peter Bergman, Tristan Rogers, and Theo Penghlis" (soap characters).

"I'm thirteen years old and my favorite soaps are 'As the World Turns' and 'The Guiding Light'."

"I'm twelve years old and I especially like Tristan Rogers and Rick Springfield (soap characters). They're cool."

"I'm eleven and I watch the ABC soaps. My favorites are 'All My Children' and 'General Hospital'."

Children who watch the soaps habitually may do so with or without their parents' knowledge. In many American households, television is watched without discrimination.

The average American household viewed an estimated six hours and forty-four minutes of television each day during the 1980-81 season, the highest season average ever reported by the A. C. Nielson ratings. This was a nine-minute-per-day increase over the previous period. But while Americans may be watching at record levels, they are viewing less network television in the prime-time evening hours. The report states that the networks now share only eighty-one percent of the prime-time audience, an all time low and a drop of three "share points" from the previous season.1

Nevertheless, overall viewing has increased steadily. The gain comes from pay-cable services and broadcast signals of major independents and superstations.

The survey also found that as of January 1982, 8.2 million homes own at least one TV. This represents an expansion of .43 million over the previous year. More than half of these homes have more than one set, and eighty-six percent own color models. The report adds that although, on the average, a household watches nearly fifty hours of television each week, families of three or more and those with children tune in for about sixty hours. Generally, women view more than men.

The average American child from six to sixteen years is viewing between twenty and twenty-four hours of television a week. This same child will spend 15,000 hours in school between grades one and twelve, and at the same time, watches 18,000 hours of television. Physical activity is vital to a young growing body and mind. Yet children are allowed to become involved in a passive activity which influences them greatly.

Children have a great capacity to suspend belief. They believe what they see and become engrossed in the make-believe games that they play and in the stories they read or see on the screen. It is more difficult for them to distinguish between reality and fantasy than it is for an adult. If some adults have trouble deciding between real life and that which is portrayed on the soaps, imagine the problem children have!

The violence, critical illness, and death depicted on the dramas can frighten children. It is so easy for

Those Sensational Soaps

them to put themselves in the place of the person being shot, drowned, or dying on the operating table. They become anxious for their own safety as well as their family's.

The strife and confrontation between the characters on the soaps can also disturb a child's home security. The young person sees a woman much like his mother and a man similar to his father arguing, accusing one another, and maybe even separating. He becomes anxious, thinking that this could happen at *his* house.

On the other hand, the child can also witness an unrealistic resolution of problems and not understand. Recently, a little girl watched a soap in which one of the characters was confined to a wheelchair. In typical soap opera fashion, she made a miraculous recovery and within days was walking. This excited the girl and gave her unqualified hopes. Her own mother was crippled by cerebral palsy, sat in a wheelchair, and would never walk again.

Blatant sexuality is another aspect of today's soap operas which affects children. Soap characters move from partner to partner and from bed to bed, often without the benefit of a marriage ceremony. They have frank discussions with one another about sexual adequacy, inadequacy, and aberrations. Children watch wide-eyed, with no interference from their parents. Yet when a note comes home from school, stating that Billy or Jane is going to be enrolled in a "sex education class," these same parents get upset and fight to get sex education out of grade school. "My child is too young to be exposed to sex," they cry.

The value system—or, perhaps, the lack of one—shown on the soap operas, is absorbed innocently by the children watching them. In spite of this fact, many parents, such as Jonathan's mother, use the television as a babysitter. Anything to keep the children quiet and out of mischief.

I like the advice given by John P. Murray, a psychologist, and Barbara Lonnborg of Nebraska's Boys Town Center: "Rather than randomly checking to see what's on, use a program guide to plan how much TV and which programs the kids should see. To control the influence of TV violence, parents can explain how and why it was faked, how they feel about violence and other ways of resolving conflicts. To help the child understand that the TV world isn't like the real world, compare TV programs to real-life experiences, showing how they differ."[3]

A dominant force affecting husbands, wives and children, soap operas strike at the center of American life—the family. If marriage and sexual relationships are important in real life, they are overwhelmingly prominent in soap operas. Courtship, marriage, and divorce are the three most essential phases in the lifecycle of a soap opera character which may be repeated again and again.

Because of this, many women who habitually watch soap operas are having serious marital difficulties. "Shouldn't they be experts on the causes of marital problems and their solutions?" you might ask. "Isn't that what the soaps are all about?" Not really. As one

Those Sensational Soaps

woman said:

> I used to watch some soaps in Spanish and spent about five hours a day. I thought they were interesting, and I could put myself in the place of the girls that had what I didn't have at home: love, money, a handsome husband, and everything a woman could dream of. Because of these soap operas, I felt frustrated, cheated and used to fight with my husband because he wasn't the kind of man that the soap opera put into my mind. The soap operas induced me to commit all kinds of sins and adultery in my mind.

Although divorce has become more and more common, the divorce statistics on the soap operas are unbelievable. A secure married life on a soap is unheard of. Courtship is unpredictable and dramatic, and divorces are also, because these are the stuff soaps are made of. A happy and secure marriage may be wonderful in real life, but it doesn't produce a successful soap opera. In every soap marriage, no matter how idyllic, the spector of divorce is always present, because with that uncertainty there is drama. A romance with another person is always right around the corner for a soap character.

But what about the soap opera viewer? What effect does this approach have on her or him? Many viewers experience a negative impact on their marriages. For one thing, it takes a great amount of time to "keep up" with the soaps. A person who spends four or five hours a day in front of the television has that much less time for creative activities, for learning and participating, for housekeeping, and for personal grooming. A woman's self-esteem suffers when these things slide, and her husband begins to notice. In many couples' counseling sessions, when the wife is a regular soap viewer, the husband complains about her involvement with the programs, her unkempt personal appearance, and the disorganized condition of the home.

Another difficulty is the comparisons made with life as it's shown on the screen. A soap viewer sees a handsome, well-dressed couple living in an elegant home and compares it to her own life. The anger and frustration she feels at being "cheated" of all this is ultimately directed toward her husband. She resents him for not being the debonair, charming, wealthy man she admires on TV. Her self-esteem erodes further because she is not the beautiful and stylish woman on the soap. Since she is convinced of the reality of these people, it doesn't occur to her that she is comparing a real-life situation to a facade. She will often tear her own marriage apart in order to keep the fantasy intact.

Since many woman who are hooked on soap operas have a problem communicating with others, it is not surprising that they also experience difficulty talking with their husbands. With so much attention focused on unreal people and situations, these women often cannot face the real problems and decisions which need discussion in any marriage. Soap stars seemingly don't make house payments, deal with car repairs, or have limited food budgets. Therefore, many viewers prefer not to deal with these real life problems, choosing instead to resent, scorn or simply ignore them. The time spent watching the soaps, and the mental preoccupation with them even when not watching, makes real communication extremely difficult.

Soap opera drama can also have negative effects on morality within real life marriages. As Katzman has pointed out, "... these shows have great potential power. They can establish or reinforce value systems. They can suggest how people should act in certain situations. They can legitimate behavior and remove taboos...."[4] In the soap opera value system, adultery, fornication, divorce, blackmail, lying and cheating are everyday occurrences. The "best" people by soap opera standards are involved in these things. Although changes have been made in the value systems of Americans over the last few decades, soap operas are not responsible for *all* those transformations. They have, however, had a forceful effect on the personal values and conduct of many viewers.

When a woman is living a great deal of her life through the drama of soaps, it is not surprising that this distorted morality becomes part of her own system of values. If one is bored in marriage, adultery begins to seem acceptable. Divorce appears to be the only alternative in marital disagreements when communication and working things through becomes burdensome.

5

"Help Me! Dr. Katz"

5

Do soap operas have a negative effect on the physical well-being of viewers as well? Proponents of these dramas hold that soaps can and do provide a public service by educating the public regarding illness and other social problems. They point to the direction taken by a legendary soap opera creator, Agnes Nixon. As head writer for "The Guiding Light" in 1964, Nixon broke ground with a bold and unprecedented story line in which a major character learns she has uterine cancer. She felt strongly that bringing life-saving information to the audience was something that the soaps could do well.

As she put it, "The ostriches among the viewers will turn off the American Cancer Society blurb or a documentary because it frightens them, but if Bert Bauer (on "The Guiding Light") or Ruth Martin (on "All My Children") have something and go to the doctor, they understand it. It's like their sister or a dear friend."[1]

Gary Deeb, a TV/radio critic and columnist, agrees with Nixon. He points out that:

Those Sensational Soaps

Social issues ranging from alcoholism and drug abuse to unemployment and the Vietnam War have been explored—usually thoughtfully—by the daytime serials.... Nixon and some of her colleagues long have realized that daytime soaps can incorporate crucial information without losing the basic elements of television entertainment.... That's been the basic spirit of the best of the soaps, including Nixon's current baby, "All My Children" on ABC. Characters come to recognize their problems over long and credible periods of time and then work them out in logical, humane ways. (On the other hand, the worst of the soaps, ABC's "General Hospital," employs mental and physical diseases only as expedient devices to keep the plot going.)[2]

Susan O'Leary, who has a doctorate in French literature and is a fellow in the woman's studies program at the University of Wisconsin, agrees with this thinking, but takes it one step further. She'd like to see the soaps offer follow-up information to viewers who have similar problems to those viewed on the air. A life-long follower and expert on the soaps, Ms. O'Leary asserts that if the soaps and the networks provided pamphlets explaining what causes the problem and how help can be obtained, they would be completing "the circle of communication" that involves the writers, producers, actors and viewers of daytime soaps. O'Leary presented her idea to the NBC, ABC, and CBS networks. NBC and ABC were not interested, but the CBS serial, "The Young and the Restless" is considering the idea.[3]

"Help Me! Dr. Katz"

Not everyone, however, agrees with Deeb that the soaps explore the characters' problems with realism and sensitivity. In an article in *Psychology Today,* Dr. Phillip DeMuth, a clinical psychologist and psychotherapist, and Dr. Elizabeth Barton, a counselor, take issue with the idea that soap operas help viewers see their own problems competently diagnosed and dealt with. Showing a typical "professional" approach to psychological counseling in soap opera style, they wrote:

> Heather enters her therapist's office for her regular appointment. With a glance verging on contempt, Dr. Katz looks up from the fishing lure he is tying. "Hello, Heather," he says, hardly pausing in his task.
> "Dr. Katz, I'm really ready to work today."
> With no effort to restrain his impatience, Katz retorts, "Come off it, Heather. Who do you think you're kidding? You're a manipulator — you know it, and I know it!"
> "But, Dr. Katz," Heather pleads, "I really mean it...."
> "I've had it with you, Heather!"
> Who would go to see a therapist like this? Approximately thirteen million people. Dr. Sy Katz is the presiding therapist on "General Hospital," television's top-rated daytime soap opera, and among television psychiatrists, his sledgehammer behavior is not exceptional.
> While television glamorizes other professions — lawyers, journalists and surgeons — it almost invariably caricatures therapists to the point of ridicule.
> In the above scene, Dr. Katz appears to be employ-

Those Sensational Soaps

ing a mutant of Gestalt therapy, reminiscent of Fritz Perls in his more forgettable moments. The therapeutic strategy is to "confront" the patient, provoking him to anger. Then the therapist pulls back and congratulates the patient on getting in touch with his "real" feelings. Dr. Katz uses this technique with great relish.[4]

And what of Deeb's claim that the characters on the soaps "come to recognize their problems over long and credible periods of time?" Drs. DeMuth and Barton offer this proof to the contrary:

> ...Ann, a nurse and co-worker of Dr. Katz, comes to him because she is upset that everyone at the hospital is covering up for a surgeon whose negligence has killed a patient. In a barrage of questions, Dr. Katz uncovers the further fact that Ann is a virgin, unable to get close to any man. He needs only five minutes to shift her attention from the first problem to the second. Clearly, he is an expert in Albert Ellis's rational-emotive therapy, too.[5]

Of course, Dr. Katz's practice is confined to "General Hospital," which Deeb has characterized as "the worst of the soaps." But "All My Children," described by Deeb as one of the "best of the soaps" has to handle its share of Barton-DeMuth criticism:

> Counterparts of Dr. Katz—we might call them Soap Opera Attending Psychotherapists or SOAPS—appear on almost every major daytime

"Help Me! Dr. Katz"

series and their nighttime equivalents. "All My Children" offers an example of instant hypnoanalysis in the healing manipulations of Dr. Marcus Polk. Donna, a hysteric, has suffered for years from emotional problems. Under hypnosis, Dr. Polk deftly leads her back to her childhood. Suddenly she remembers that her father had raped her. This startling insight, achieved in perhaps fifteen minutes, cures Donna once and for all.[6]

If the therapy that soap opera characters undergo is unrealistic, the problems which necessitate it are even more so:

> ...No more likely...are the emotional problems that the soaps must heal. Psychotherapists will testify to the low incidence in real life of such disorders as multiple personality, hysterical pregnancy, or dissociative amnesia. Their incidence in the soap cities of Llanview ("One Life to Live"), Port Charles ("General Hospital") and Genoa City ("The Young and the Restless") defies national statistics.
> Split personalities also proliferate. It all began nine years ago on "One Life to Live," when Vickie was given two lives to live: Vickie the Saint and Nickie the Sinner. The contagion quickly spread through the airways to the other shows. The patients are always women, and they always have a good half and a bad half. On "Days of Our Lives," for example, Jesse studies in a convent by day, but comes out as Angie the hooker by night. In such cases the therapists earn their pay, fusing the two halves. The good half always prevails.[7]

Those Sensational Soaps

Soap viewers are treated to more than a nodding acquaintance with a variety of emotional illnesses and professional treatment of those ills. But Drs. DeMuth and Barton strongly disagree with the premise that viewers are actually *informed* by the soaps. Rather, they contend, they are being misinformed, and the soaps are performing a public disservice.

They point, for example, to the treatment of the Masters and Johnson sex therapy on "The Guiding Light":

> ...In one episode...internist Sara McIntyre simply announces that she is a sex therapist, and before long she has a thriving practice, with every woman on the show signed up for sessions. Invariably, each comes without husband or boyfriend, which makes soap opera sense, as neither Sara nor the patients ever suggest that sexual problems are anything but a woman's fault. Sara never recommends that her patients tell their partners about receiving sex therapy, and the obliging women keep the "embarrassing" secret to themselves.[8]

The misinformation that abounds on the soaps is more likely to confuse people about counseling and therapy than bring them "life-saving information." Voicing their concern, Drs. DeMuth and Barton conclude:

> Freud feared that our unwillingness to face ourselves would be the downfall of psychoanalysis. It may be the case that uninformed viewers are being

"Help Me! Dr. Katz"

dissuaded from therapy by its soap opera portrayal.[9]

Soap opera illnesses allow many opportunities for drama. Along with all the psychological problems which plague characters, many physical problems trouble them as well. After the diagnosis of the illness, the soap character often will deny the report and attempt to hide the fact that he or she is suffering from heart disease, brain tumor, or progressive blindness. Minor illnesses are rare on soaps, and fortunately, each individual has several intimate friends who are members of the medical profession. These doctors and nurses are not only diagnosticians, but also detectives. They stay on the trail of their patient-friends until the illness is admitted to and treatment begins.

The treatment, which almost invariably requires hospitalization and surgery, also provides drama. The operation is usually high-risk and rarely goes smoothly. The patient must have at least one life-or-death crisis in the course of the illness, and some have several. Since the hospital is staffed by friends of the patient, many visits between patient, friends and family occur. Miraculously, within a few days of having a foot in death's door, the patient is again radiant, fashionably dressed, and out on the town.

Although the "medical" soaps, such as "General Hospital" and "The Doctors," are greatly peopled with disease-prone characters, the other dramas also have more than their share. As critics have often pointed out, the medical statistics on soap operas defy national norms. With all the romantic entanglements,

Those Sensational Soaps

the soaps exceed their per capita quota of pregnancies. But the births rarely occur without complications. Rose Goldsen, in an article on the subject, reported the following statistics for the first half of 1975:

> Eleven pregnancies produced two miscarriages, two abortions under consideration, two births almost fatal to the mother, a third premature delivery that took place during a blizzard without qualified medical assistance. (The soaps) lost only one mother in the year's first half. That was poor Addie Williams who died just after being delivered of Baby Hope, who survived. Addie dies not of the terminal cancer she was suffering from, nor from the complications to be expected when a grandmother goes through pregnancy. She was killed in a car accident. ("Days of our Lives")[10]

The sickness and suffering shown on the soaps have a negative effect on even the most cheerful, optimistic viewer. If a person who watches a great deal of TV soaps has problems with depression, the unhealthiness of the soaps may well breed even more despondency. Many reports from women verify that after seeing an illness vividly described and treated on the dramas, they begin to believe that they have some of the symptoms.

An interesting story was related by a woman I'll call Helen. A regular soap viewer, Helen was having problems with her husband. When he was sober, he worked hard and provided a good home. But he had

"Help Me! Dr. Katz"

a problem with alcohol. Although she tried hard to help him conquer the habit, nothing worked, and the problem continued to weigh heavily upon her. She went often to discuss the situation with her pastor, but the problem seemed insurmountable.

Helen's favorite soap opera was "All My Children." On the program Palmer Cortlandt, one of the characters, was found guilty of plotting the murder of Sybil. In reaction to this verdict, Cortlandt was struck with a severe case of amnesia.

Helen was impressed by this reaction to adversity and wished that she could make her problems go away so completely. Within days, she had to contact her doctor for treatment of what seemed to be a worsening case of amnesia. Instead, the doctor diagnosed it as a bad case of fantasy. Lynda Hersch, a syndicated columnist who reports a weekly summary of soap opera plots, has said, "You're not an official soap opera character until you've had amnesia."[11]

Although doctors are familiar with the power of suggestion and its effects on psychosomatic illnesses, women who are thoroughly immersed in the soaps often do not take their symptoms, psychosomatic or otherwise, to their family physician. They doubt their own doctor's competency, but rarely question the qualifications of the physicians on "General Hospital" or "The Doctors." They watch avidly, hoping to find the diagnosis and cure for their ailments.

In 1941 a psychiatrist from New York, Dr. Louis Berg, began a crusade against soap operas. He believed they had a dangerous influence on those suffering from neuroses, particularly adolescents and middle-aged persons. For the unfortunates who were addicted to them, the soaps provided, as Dr. Berg put it, "the same release for the emotionally distorted that is supplied to those who derive satisfaction from a lynching bee, who lick their lips at the salacious scandals of a crime passional, who in the unregretted past cried out in ecstasy at a witch burning."[12]

He set out to test his hypothesis that such symptoms as tachycardia (excessively rapid heartbeat), arrhythmia (irregularity of heartbeat), vertigo (a sensation of dizziness; a confused, disoriented state of mind), and emotional instability might be produced by soap operas. Included in his study were some tests he performed using himself as a guinea pig. After listening to two popular radio soaps, "Right to Happiness" and "Woman in White," he examined his blood pressure and discovered that it had risen significantly. As a result of his research, he concluded that soaps can cause real problems for certain people when listened to habitually.[13]

Although psychiatrists and social scientists have not given a great deal of attention to the soaps, some interesting research has been conducted. Dr. David P. Phillips, a sociologist at the University of California in San Diego, has linked suicides on TV soaps to the actual suicide rate. Dr. Phillips presented the first systematic evidence indicating that violent, fictional television stories trigger imitative deaths and near-fatal accidents in the United States.[14]

In 1977 an increase of at least 127 suicides and 161

motor vehicle fatalities was reported immediately following soap opera suicide stories. After allowing for non-fictional suicide stories, linear trends, and seasonal and day-of-the-week fluctuations in the data, the increases are statistically significant.

Female suicides, single-vehicle fatalities, and single-vehicle nonfatal accidents increased after the soap suicide stories aired. This growth apparently occurred because soap suicides trigger imitative suicides and suicide attempts, some of which are disguised as single-vehicle accidents.

Dr. Phillips contends that the increase in female suicides is of course to be expected, since women watch more soap operas than men. The fact that urban residents responded more strongly than nonurban dwellers was not predicted, however. It is easy to speculate, but no conclusive explanation for this finding is presently available. Any such conclusion must take into account the different viewing patterns of urban and nonurban residents. Information on this subject is available to commercial sponsors of television programs, but does not seem to be freely accessible to academic researchers. In the absence of such data, it would be premature to consider this urban/nonurban disparity.

Dr. Phillips, who is not a soap fan, cautions that further research is needed to *prove* the correlation between soap opera suicides and the actual suicide rate. Although suicide is an extreme action, other less startling behavior patterns, which are also self-destructive, are often the result of habitual soap watching.

# 6

Sensational or Sinsational?

6

Why are these daily dramas so appealing and addictive? How can a person deal with soap opera addiction? Is this a problem only among women who have no religious background, or do women of the church become hooked on soaps? If a Christian is under the influence of soap operas, how can the habit be overcome?

Determined to find answers to these questions, I formulated a survey about soap operas and sent copies to approximately 1,500 women all over the United States. Because the surveys were distributed through churches of various denominations, the responses received were generally from women who had some church affiliation. They were asked which shows they watched and how often. I also queried, "Why do you watch the soaps?" and "If you once viewed them and you no longer do, what made you stop?"

Of the 1,500 survey sheets distributed, 1,011 were returned. The results were amazing. More than forty-

Those Sensational Soaps

nine percent of the respondents watched the soaps regularly. The most popular programs were "General Hospital" and "One Life to Live." "All My Children" and "As the World Turns" tied for third place.

The women who watch the soaps reported forty-six occupations, including housewives, secretaries, nurses, minister's wives, beauticians, cashiers, missionaries and waitresses. The majority were between the ages of eighteen and forty-nine, and a low percentage were in the fifty and over age group.

In most cases, women who once watched the soaps but no longer did, and women who have never watched the soaps wrote long, well-thought-out comments on the survey. But those who regularly watched several daily dramas seemed unable to formulate a logical, concise response to the question, "Why do you watch the soaps?" A high percentage of women who were divorced and stayed at home with children viewed three to four hours of the dramas a day.

The survey also indicated that the nighttime soaps had a vast viewing audience which included men, women, teenagers, and children. The number one evening soap was "Dallas."

Many of the answers to "Why do you watch soap operas?" were straightforward and predictable:

"They keep me company."

"There is nothing else on at the time and I don't like to read."

"I enjoy them while I relax."

Sensational or Sinsational?

"I watch the soaps just for the fun of it and to see what's going on."

"They are a tremendous pastime."

But some of the answers seem to point to problems from which the respondent is trying to escape:

"I watch soap operas when I get depressed and don't want to communicate with anyone. I also watch them when I am spiritually low."

Depression seems to be a typical problem of soap watchers. One wonders why a person who feels depressed would turn to the soaps, of all places, for comfort. The characters in the dramas certainly have more confusion, turmoil, and unhappiness in their lives than most real people have in theirs. A woman from California explained it saying, "I watch soap operas because they show other people's lives are always worse than mine."

Perhaps the traumas and turmoil of the soaps offer reassurance to some, but to the majority of women who returned the survey, the soaps were depressing:

I watch some soap operas, and I find them very depressing to my mind and also to my spirit."

"Soap operas are very depressing, and they set a mood that causes fantasies with a person's real life."

"I have watched them for ten years.... I know they are depressing."

Those Sensational Soaps

The negative effects of the soaps can be attributed to several causes. The constant string of troubles which ensnares the characters – the illnesses, accidents, murders, deaths, and divorces – are depressing. But the other side of the soap opera coin – the glamor, wealth, elegance, romance – can also be extremely depressing to someone whose life contains little of those things. As many of those surveyed admitted:

> "Watching the soaps has caused a great deal of frustration in my life. I have compared the life of my family and myself to what I have seen on the TV."
>
> "The soaps made me so unsatisfied with my life that I tried several times to take my own life."

Another contributing cause of depression is the physical, mental, and social inactivity which comes from watching hours of soaps each day. They prevent frequent viewers from accomplishing things that would strengthen their self-esteem. One woman revealed:

> "I watch the soaps during the day as I work nights.... I have tried to stop watching them as they cause me to get so far behind on my work, but my mind won't let me."

Another said:

> "Soaps demand my time, my home, my husband, and my family."

Sensational or Sinsational?

Several who responded to the survey noted the negative effect watching the soaps has had on their marriages. One person acknowledged:

> "I became hooked on soaps and played the part of one of the stars. I ruined my marriage."

Knowing all the hazards of viewing soap operas, why do women still watch them? Simply because they are *addicted* to soaps. As Carol said in her story, "I was hooked on them...like an alcoholic or one who has been on drugs." This confession was echoed by many of the women when they admitted:

> "I know they are addictive...I watch them because I can't help myself."
>
> "I would give anything if I could stop watching them."
>
> "They waste my time. My imagination needs to be controlled, but I'm hooked on them."
>
> "I do not want them to control my life or my thinking. I am having a battle."
>
> "...For nineteen years I have been addicted to the soap operas. I went to work once and stopped, but have found myself caught up in the ensnarement again...I could get hooked very bad again. I do not want to do that."

Troubled people seek escape from their worries, search for a way to feel good again, and desire comfort and peace. Some turn to drugs, some to alcohol,

Those Sensational Soaps

and others to soap operas. For many the solution to their problems becomes a problem in itself. Yet many soap opera addicts do see the conflict between their Christian principles and the values portrayed in the soaps:

> "Soap operas are very possessive and made me very emotional in an ungodly way. They really made me lust, I am ashamed to say."
>
> "Soaps glamorize lust, infidelity, unwholesome attitudes, and cause me to have a hardened heart. I know all of that, but I still watch them."
>
> "It (soap watching) is a downgrading of biblical principles as you are constantly feeding the mind with unacceptable behavior, divorce, murder and other affairs. I would give anything if I could stop watching them."

Finding it difficult to break the soap opera habit, they have taken a step forward by examining the moral implications of the programs. Many addicted Christian women, however, have not yet made that effort. Instead, they still see soaps as "innocent entertainment."

When I undertook my research and viewed "All My Children" one hour a day for twenty days, I took notes as I watched. Within that time span, thirty-nine sins which the Bible mentions were committed. And this was only *one* soap! A scanning of *Soap Opera Digest,* which provides a weekly summary of all the plots, shows a similar story line on *all* the programs.

Sensational or Sinsational?

The Bible says, "But let none of you suffer as a murderer, or a thief, or any sort of criminal; or as a mischief-maker (a meddler) in the affairs of others — infringing on their rights."[1] Yet, a sampling of soap plots indicates that murder is commonplace. Mr. Cortlandt of "All My Children" had Sybil murdered. In "Another World" Loretta died under suspicious circumstances, and Harry suspected Steve of murder. On "Ryan's Hope," China gave Orson the order to kill Joe. Packy was shot by one of Darnley's men on "General Hospital" — and on it goes. Murder is the routine way to take care of enemies on the soaps.

Theft is commonplace, too. Petty thievery happens often, but more dramatic theft occurs also. On "The Doctors," for example, Dennis and Frankie robbed a grave in the Aldrich crypt. And thieves stole from thieves during an episode of "General Hospital," when Blackie thwarted a mugger on the way home from his mother's funeral. He then stole the attackers ill-gotten money so he could pay for her burial. Thus, the soaps justify robbery, saying that it is a "have to" case when people steal to take care of a need. But God says any theft is wrong.

And where would soap operas be without the sin of meddling? Each soap has one or several characters who keep the plot simmering by interfering in the private lives of others. Erica on "All My Children" meddles constantly in her brother Mark's life and also in Silver's. Renee in "Days of Our Lives" operates in the same way. Destructive meddling in love affairs, money matters, and family situations is common on

Those Sensational Soaps

the programs.

The Apostle Paul wrote to the Christians in the church of Ephesus:

> But immorality (sexual vice) and all impurity [of lustful, rich, wasteful living] or greediness must not even be named among you, as is fitting and proper among saints (God's consecrated people).
> Let there be no filthiness, (obscenity, indecency) nor foolish and sinful (silly and corrupt) talk, nor coarse jesting, which are not fitting or becoming; but instead voice your thankfulness [to God].
> For be sure of this, that no person practicing sexual vice or impurity in *thought* or in life, or one who is covetous — that is, who has lustful desire for the property of others and is greedy for gain — [for] that [in effect] is an idolater, has any inheritance in the kingdom of Christ and of God.[2]

These are powerful words, exhorting the Christian to avoid the lusts of the flesh which the soaps elaborate — immorality, wasteful living, greed, foolish and corrupt talk, covetousness and lustful desires.

Illicit love is plentiful on "The Young and the Restless," as Paul romances Cindy, who is a hooker at the Golden Touch, and on "General Hospital," with Noah and Tiffany so much in love, they run off to Cannes together. Adultery and fornication are highlighted by joy, happiness and emotional excitement. Romantic affairs flourish in lavish surroundings, and the dialogue is witty and wonderful. A typical plot concerns the handsome husband with a lovely wife

Sensational or Sinsational?

and children who goes to his mistress's house. Everything is beautiful as he sweeps her off her feet with embraces, kisses and sweet words. Passionately, he carries her up the winding stairs into the bedroom. Although in the next instant, the viewer sees the bare back of the woman and the sexy, hairy chest of the man, the actual sex act is not shown. His imagination, however, completes the scene, and he smiles approval, yearning for the same experience.

The Bible calls such "entertainment" *sin* and indicates that it destroys the soul. "But when you follow your own wrong inclinations your lives will produce these evil results: impure thoughts, eagerness for lustful pleasure, idolatry, spiritism (that is, encouraging the activity of demons), hatred and fighting, jealousy and anger, constant effort to get the best for yourself, complaints and criticisms, the feeling that everyone else is wrong except those in your own little group — and there will be wrong doctrine, envy, murder, drunkenness, wild parties, and all that sort of thing. Let me tell you again as I have before, that anyone living that sort of life will not inherit the kingdom of God."[3]

Since people remember eighty percent of what they see and hear, the viewer who is addicted to soap operas, begins to think, act, say and feel what the soaps teach. As the slow moving story lines register deep within his mind, he is often able to recall soap happenings even from previous years. Through such indoctrination, Christian soap watchers are being cheated and deceived. They believe they are watching

Those Sensational Soaps

inexpensive entertainment, but instead the lust of the flesh is tearing down their thinking abilities and lowering their moral standards.

Anger is another rampant emotion on the soaps, and bitter words are frequent. The distraught Matt blasts Carolee on "The Doctors," and his obscenity offends all who hear him. In the following story line from "The Guiding Light," two brothers Ross and Justin, exchange angry threats and accusations:

> Justin tries to convince Ross that he told the truth about Carrie. But Ross screams angrily that he is lying about the woman he loves and trusts. Justin grabs Ross's arm and begs for a chance to explain, but he yanks free and dashes for the elevator. As the doors close, Justin desperately warns his brother to listen to Sara for Carrie's sake. Ross shouts back that he is tired of Justin's lies and phony concern for the sister-in-law that he tried to seduce behind his back. Thus, Justin realizes that Carrie must know that Phillip is really his and Jackie's son, and is threatening Jackie with the information.

One sin leads to another as dissensions, anger, strife, hatred, selfishness, lust and fornication roll across the screen. Resentments erupt into insulting behavior which satisfies the hatred and often culminates in murder. Yet the Christian is admonished to, "let all bitterness and indignation and wrath (passion, rage, bad temper) and resentment (anger, animosity) and quarreling (brawling, clamor, contention) and slander (evilspeaking, abusive or blasphemous

Sensational or Sinsational?

language) be banished from you, with all malice (spite, ill will or baseness of any·kind)."[4]

Equally as appealing is the greed and envy, glorified in many of the soap plots. On "The Guiding Light," for example, Brian and Mark conspire to acquire the Spaulding empire, and the infamous J. R. Ewing swindles, cheats and lies to obtain voting rights to the Ewing Estate on "Dallas." They certainly prove the Scripture true which says, "He who is greedy for unjust gain troubles his own household. . . ."[5]

Kim is angry and upset on "Ryan's Hope," due to her jealousy of Amanda, and Judith in "Texas," after sneaking into George's studio, flies into a rage when she sees Reena's pictures plastered all over the walls. Continuously, husband and wife, wife and lover, husband and mistress are jealous, conceited and arrogant, often showing that "pride goes before destruction and a haughty spirit before a fall."[6]

Overindulgence in gambling and drinking greatly affects the lives of soap characters as well. On "Search for Tomorrow" Brock challenges Martin to a poker game which Martin loses. The more he loses, the more he drinks. Spending the night with Gloria, he jeopardizes his marriage to Jo and goes into debt for $25,000. He continues drinking and decides to get revenge.

The Bible warns that watching and condoning such sins is unwise. "So do not associate or be sharers with them. For once you were darkness, but now you are light in the Lord; walk as children of light — lead the lives of those native-born to the Light. Take no part

Those Sensational Soaps

in and have no fellowship with the fruitless deeds and enterprises of darkness, but instead [let your lives be so in contrast as to] expose and reprove and convict them. For it is a shame even to speak of or mention the things that [such people] practice in secret. Look carefully then how you walk! Live purposefully and worthily and accurately, not as the unwise and witless, but as wise – sensible, intelligent people; making the very most of the time – buying up each opportunity – because the days are evil."[7]

As enticing as the sins of the soaps, is the lure of their lavish surroundings. Settings include exciting parties at posh restaurants and night clubs where gourmet food, fine wine, and cocktails are served by beautiful girls. Violin music plays in the background and the aroma is divine. What woman with a touch of greed and jealousy would not desire to be entertained in such a luscious manner? Only in unusual circumstances to further the plot is the overindulgence of alcohol or boisterous merrymaking and carousing portrayed. And *never* is the mistress or lover seen chomping hamburgers at a fast-food joint!

But as Christians settle for this world of fantasy, their hope ends in disappointment. When garbage is taken into the mind, garbage has to come out. "...Do people pick grapes from thorns, or figs from thistles? Even so every healthy (sound) tree bears good fruit – worthy of admiration; but the sickly (decaying, worthless) tree bears bad and worthless fruit. A good (healthy) tree cannot bear bad (worthless) fruit; nor can a bad (diseased) tree bear excellent fruit – worthy of admiration."[8]

Sensational or Sinsational?

From the outside, a beautiful large, red apple may appear juicy and delicious. But one bite reveals its brown, decayed and rotten center. The worm has destroyed a thing of beauty from within. Jesus said, "What comes out of a man is what makes a man unclean and renders [him] unhallowed. For from within, [that is] out of the heart of men, come base and wicked thoughts: sexual immorality, stealing, murder, adultery, coveting (a greedy desire to have more wealth), dangerous and destructive wickedness, deceit; unrestrained (indecent) conduct; an evil eye (envy), slander (evil speaking, malicious misrepresentation, abusiveness); pride—[that is] the sin of an uplifted heart against God and man; foolishness (folly, lack of sense, recklessness, thoughtlessness). All these evil [purposes and desires] come from within, and they make the man unclean and render him unhallowed."[9]

Seeds of immorality, greed, hatred, strife, selfishness and anger are like the worm in the apple. Planted deep in the mind's core, these sins begin to ferment. As the worm lives, eats and exists day after day in the apple, so habitual viewing of the soaps causes sin to dwell in the mind continuously. Appearing to be shiny beautiful apples on the outside, soap viewers may pray, attend church and teach Bible studies. But inside, the worm continues to eat, live, grow and exist. And if he remains in the apple long enough, it is destroyed.

"For the time is coming when [people] will not tolerate (endure) sound and wholesome instruction, but having ears itching [for something pleasing and gratifying], they will gather to themselves one teacher after another to a considerable number, chosen to satisfy their own liking and to foster the errors they hold, and will turn aside from hearing the truth and wander off into myths and man-made fictions."[10]

The myths and man-made fictions which the soaps provide are seductive as well as addictive. According to testimonies of hundreds of Christian women, the soaps are not "just innocent entertainment." Frustrated women and men become immersed in them because they are looking for solutions to their problems, seeking freedom from depression, and desiring inner peace. But by submerging themselves in the unreality and immorality of the soaps, they receive instead more problems, more depression, and more inner turmoil. With a steady diet of sin planted in their minds and hearts, joy, peace, and true satisfaction remain elusive.

7

Bursting the Soap Bubble

7

The spider is one of God's most creative creatures, and its artistic ability has been studied by scientists throughout the world. They are amazed at the intricate design of the web, which is built mainly to secure food and protection. The outer edge is not as sticky as the inner web, and the insect that flies into it could get out if he did not become frustrated and panic. But the more the insect moves, the more he gets entangled, and soon there is no release.

Many insects get caught in the web because of curiosity. Seeking to investigate this attraction, they proceed to the center of the web, persuaded that they will conquer the spider. But little do they realize the strength of the trap. Only the largest and strongest of them overcome the snare and catch the spider.

In much the same way as the spider, soap opera authors write stories which ensnare men, woman and children. Their power with words creates a web that is so inviting to the audience that it is easy to be enticed. Those who get caught in the outer edge of the

Those Sensational Soaps

web are the viewers whose lives are filled with frustration, boredom and anxieties. "I'll watch the program and find the answer to my problems," the viewer rationalizes, thinking that he will not become hooked. But just as the spider's web holds its victim, the soap viewer does get caught. Each day he tells himself, "I won't continue to watch." Nevertheless, he becomes more attached to the sticky substance—the plot which the artistic writer has devised.

Many viewers begin watching out of curiosity, saying, "I've seen the advertisement and wonder what it is about," "My girlfriend recommended it," or "I'll look and see if it is really as bad as what I've heard." Once curiosity has been satisfied, the viewer must then convince himself that it did not hurt his spiritual life. He might hear himself saying, "It was very interesting," "The program helped me to relax," or "The actors portrayed their parts so well."

Another type of viewer decides to attack the spider—the writers, producers and advertisers. This is usually the strong Christian soap watcher who dares to fly into the middle of the web where the danger is the most potent. "Nothing can hurt me!" he declares. Lest pride be his downfall, he should beware. "Therefore let any one who thinks he stands—who feels sure that he has a steadfast mind and is standing firm—take heed lest he fall [into sin]."[1]

Justifying ourselves is not a good way to help fight the harmfulness of soap watching. Forty-nine percent of all Christian women are watching the soaps—at least two or more programs a day. If these millions

Bursting the Soap Bubble

of viewers would stop watching the dramas and cease buying the products that they advertise, soap ratings would show a definite decline. Such action would be a direct attack on the spider — the soap opera syndication.

This media web is an ensnarement designed to control the minds of those who become addicted. Satan especially uses such devices to trap the Christian, allowing him to believe that it is merely enjoyment and relaxation. Gradually through constant watching, his mind becomes numb to the acts of sin and he begins to compromise, saying "Everyone is doing it, so that makes it right." In reality, the soaps destroy the Christian's morality, his relationships — his very life.... "They conceive mischief and bring forth evil! They hatch adders' eggs, and weave the spider's web;.... Their webs will not serve as clothing, nor will they cover themselves with what they make; their works are works of iniquity, and the act of violence is in their hands."[2]

The Christian's life can be so full of the fruit of the Spirit — love, joy, peace, patience kindness, goodness and longsuffering — that there is no room for the works of the devil shown on a TV screen. If we are to be about the *Father's* business, not Satan's, can we justify wasting that many hours a day?

A person who has become addicted to soap operas is like one who has settled for eating breakfast and who has forgotten lunch and dinner. He is starved for reality and has become a victim of "soap opera thinking." The illusion that the highest good, the ultimate happiness and fulfillment can come in a relationship with another human being must be changed. And until that thinking process is transformed and healed, it will not help to stop watching the soaps. The viewer is simply stuck on that mental level and continues to feel frustrated.

I have found any soap opera addict can break this mental bondage, first by recognizing that the addiction exists and that it contributes to physical, psychological and spiritual problems. Second, by substituting positive actions, he can destroy the negative habit that drains his mental and emotional strength. Third, by practicing self-discipline, the frustrated soap watcher can create a new self-image which will help him separate fantasy from reality. And fourth, by renewing his mind to the Word of God, the victimized viewer can create a high life-style, impregnated with creative, mental, emotional and spiritual power. When the Christian is ready to admit, "The soaps do not edify my spiritual life," he has already begun to conquer the addiction. Deliverance for the child of God begins with the acknowledgment of the gap between what God's Word says and what the eye sees. As one overcomer testified:

> "I used to watch 'All My Children' but was delivered from it after I accepted the Lord as Savior. Once I became born again I found the answer to my life of turmoil. I looked at this program with new eyes, and for the first time I saw all the ugliness and negative things in the soap."

Bursting the Soap Bubble

Carol in her earlier testimony verified that a release from bondage *is* possible, saying:

> "...I don't know what gave me the ability to stop watching them except God's grace. I was so bad. I was hooked on them. For some reason God had mercy on me and gave me extra strength to do what I had to do....Once the Lord frees you from something you don't want to go back to it."

Women who come for counseling often admit that they have problems in their marriage and family. But the dilemma is blamed on someone else—husband, children, in-laws. These women possess a vague sense of guilt about watching the soaps, and the time it takes from their children and housekeeping. Although they are concerned over the "terrible" things that happen on the programs, it's nothing that they examine closely. It is only when the viewer becomes aware of the fruitlessness and darkness which the soaps produce, that she is able to initiate a commitment to be free of their influence.

One woman who was a daily soap watcher had never realized that the content of the soaps contradicted the Christian principles she believed in. On one occasion, however, it was made clear to her, when a soap-watching friend had to miss one afternoon because of an emergency. When her friend arrived home, she called to learn what had happened on the programs that day. Eagerly, the woman explained to her soap after soap—telling of the man who began an af-

Those Sensational Soaps

fair with his brother's wife, the blackmail plot against the boss by the employee who knew of his gambling and his visits to a call girl, a doctor's plan to murder with a drug overdose the teenager who was carrying his baby. "I realized then how rotten it all is," she admitted. Repeating the stories aloud helped her to comprehend the luridness of the shows she was absorbing and encouraged her to do something about her addiction.

After recognizing the addiction, the Christian through practicing self-discipline can begin to replace the negative habit with positive action. Carol explained what she had to do to conquer her addiction, saying, "It was hard. I had to unplug the TV, go outside, and plan things away from home when the soaps were on... I began to fill my life with positive things to replace the negatives of the soaps. This took much discipline. I went back to school and made sure to fill my life with positive things to replace the void of the soaps." As we begin to experience the Christian reality, the fantasies of the soaps pale in comparison.

Jane was another Christian who found this to be true. Recounting her story, she said:

> I was sixteen years old when I started watching the soaps. I got out of school early, and at lunch time I would turn on the TV and watch "All My Children." There I saw a cute guy whose name was Phil. Tara was his girlfriend. I started getting interested in Phil and Tara with all of their struggles of everyday life. From that point on, I was hooked on the soaps.
>
> After high school I got a job, and during my lunch

Bursting the Soap Bubble

hour, I would run over to the Broadway store, stand in front of the TV eating my lunch and watch "All My Children." At that time in my life, that soap was the only one I was hooked on. Later in life, becoming bored and depressed, I began to watch soap operas all day long, including "All My Children," "One Life to Live," and "General Hospital." Those were my favorites.

When I started watching the soap operas, I was a Christian and didn't think there was anything wrong with them. The day became filled with soaps. I couldn't do the housework before the soap operas, so I would not get my work done. I took the phone off the hook and sometimes did not answer it. I wouldn't answer the door because it made me so mad to have my concentration interrupted.

I had a two-year-old and a five-year-old, and I remember yelling at them trying to get them to be quiet. I would do just about anything to keep them quiet and busy, so that I could see what was happening on the soaps.

The soaps took priority over everything. When my husband came home once in a while at lunchtime, I would get terribly upset at him, because I had to stop watching and fix his lunch. While eating, my husband and my children were without conversation, because I was too mad to talk. My husband didn't go along with the idea of my watching the soaps. Several times when something bad or ugly would happen, he cautioned me about letting the small children see such happenings. My husband didn't think it was good for the kids. He thought the soaps were kind of dumb and never wanted me to watch them. He didn't force me to stop watching them, but he told me how stupid

Those Sensational Soaps

they were. I wouldn't listen to him, and this caused many problems.

All morning I thought about the actions of the various characters, and often at night I dreamed about the soap situations. They were a controlling force in my life.

I am now twenty-seven years old, and in the last four years, I have begun to feel it was wrong to watch the soaps. I was under such conviction. I felt like I had to give them up, but every time I tried to stop, it would only last for just a few days. Then I would be right back watching them again.

I justified myself so that the conviction I felt inside would not bother me. I told myself, "I'll only watch Jenny and Greg on 'All My Children.' They are having so many struggles, and as soon as it all gets straightened out, then I'll stop watching."

But with the soaps it doesn't occur that way, because the writers keep things happening so that the viewer continues watching. When you think in your mind that you will stop at a certain point, you don't. I even attended a soap opera workshop that was held in Los Angeles at a church convention. Afterwards, for a short time I did really well in not watching. But soon I was trapped again.

After some time, I realized why I went back to watching the soaps. It is so simple, and yet so many get tricked by Satan who makes us think that everything is OK. The thing lacking in my life was spending time with the Lord each day. I did not study and read God's Word, and spend any time talking with the Lord. I was not letting Him fill the capacity that makes one content.

Bursting the Soap Bubble

Jane and Carol had much in common because they began watching soaps as a pastime. Gradually, as circumstances changed and problems appeared, the soaps became their escape. Soap fantasies became reality to them; they were hooked. They failed to heed the advice to: "...avoid all empty (vain, useless, idle) talk, for it will lead people into more and more ungodliness. And their teaching [will devour; it] will eat its way like cancer or spread like gangrene... For among them are those who worm their way into homes and captivate silly and weak-natured and spiritually dwarfed women, loaded down with [the burden of their] sins, [and easily] swayed and led away by various evil desires and seductive impulses. [These weak women will listen to anybody who will teach them]; they are forever inquiring and getting information, but are never able to arrive at a recognition and knowledge of the Truth."[3] Eventually each woman overcame the problem by turning to the Lord for light and strength and acting upon her belief that deliverance was assured.

Lest one gains the impression that soap opera addiction is something that happens to "someone else," let me tell the story of one other woman—me! A licensed minister with advanced courses in psychology and sociology, I have counseled many women who have had problems with soap opera addictions. Therefore, I never believed that the soaps could tempt *me* in any way. When I became aware of what an insidious problem this addiction was and decided to learn more about it, I didn't know my work

Those Sensational Soaps

was cut out for me. I had never watched a soap opera! I knew a lot *of* them, but had no first-hand knowledge.

I decided to watch "All My Children" for a month. Since this was aired for one hour at noon, I could easily fit it into my schedule by viewing it on my lunch break. I told my secretary what I was doing and instructed her that I was not to be bothered for the hour.

Each day I observed Erica and Brandon, a married man with two children, in their wild love affair, while Brandon's daughter tried desperately to pry them apart. I watched Mr. Cortlandt scheme to have Sybil murdered and fix the blame on his son-in-law, whom he hated. I sat with pen in hand, notebook and Bible by my side, not really knowing at the time what I was looking for.

My goal was to view twenty hours of soaps — enough, I thought, for me to gather some firsthand knowledge of them. About twelve days into my project, I was busy at my job one morning, when suddenly I realized that my mind was not on my work at all. Instead, I was wondering how Erica was going to win Brandon over completely, whether or not Monique was actually going to testify, and if she did, would she tell the truth! My intellect was entirely tangled in the web the soap opera had spun! I had set out to do some objective research, with good intentions, and fell into the trap that I knew perfectly well was set and waiting! The experience taught me a powerful lesson about the shocking influence of the soaps. How easy it must be for the woman who

Bursting the Soap Bubble

thinks, "They're just entertainment," to fall into the same snare. They are deceived by fixing their minds on the wrong things.

> For the rest, brethren, whatever is true, whatever is worthy of reverence and is honorable and seemly, whatever is just, whatever is pure, whatever is lovely and lovable, whatever is kind and winsome and gracious, if there is any virtue and excellence, if there is anything worthy of praise, *think on and weigh and take account of these things — fix your minds on them.*
> Practice what you have learned and received and heard and seen in me, and model your way of living on it, and the God of *peace — of untroubled, undisturbed well-being — will be with you.*[4]

It was obvious that my well-being was disturbed by watching the programs. If the mind is fixed on anxieties, immorality, and unreality, life will be modeled after those things. Therefore, if one intends to kick the habit, viewing has to be replaced with positive activity. Volunteering to work in a hospital, visiting the elderly, starting a home Bible study, and going back to school are among the many alternatives to television. But although these are effective activities, the best substitute for soap watching is fellowshiping with the Lord through prayer and meditation on His Word.

Since soap opera addiction traps the viewer in an imaginary social environment, he stops setting goals and denies the creative power that is placed there at

Those Sensational Soaps

birth. The substitute of sin has crept in, destroying valuable time, energy and physical aliveness. In His loving kindness, God challenges us to ..."Set your minds and keep them set on what is above—the higher things—not on the things that are on the earth."[5] In the power of *His* strength we are to... "test and prove all things [until you can recognize] what is good; [to that] hold fast. Abstain from evil—shrink from it and keep aloof from it—in whatever form or whatever kind it may be."[6] This can only be achieved through constant fellowship with God.

Self-fulfillment does not come with living a soap opera existence. Wearing designer clothes, dining in elegant restaurants, being wooed and won by one successful, attractive man after another does not make Reena, Erica or Samantha happy—nor can it provide lasting happiness for any soap viewer. True contentment only comes from "the God of peace, of untroubled, undisturbed well-being."

It takes strength and self-discipline to be a mature Christian. We were created in the image of God to "mount up as eagles, run and not be weary, walk and not faint."[7] What a beautiful example Christ gave us. Constant fellowship with the Lord enables us to confess, "I have strength for all things in Christ Who empowers me—I am ready for anything and equal to anything through Him Who infuses inner strength into me, [that is, I am self-sufficient in Christ's sufficiency]."[8]

And what a tremendous power He is in us. The Bible confirms, "Since you desire and seek (perceptible) proof of the Christ Who speaks in and through me. [For He] is not weak and feeble in dealing with you, but is a mighty power within you."[9] That strength is there for the asking, enabling us to grow away from the soaps and mature as Christians. With His help we will "no longer be children, tossed [like ships] to and fro between chance gusts of teaching...."[10]

God placed creative energy and ability in all of us and we are to use it for self-fulfillment and the good of others. Having the understanding and the self-discipline to do that is what Christian maturity is all about. We are cautioned to, "Be not like the horse or the mule, which lack understanding; which must have their mouths held firm with bit and bridle, else they will not come with you."[11] Yet don't the soaps do that very thing? – halter us with a bit and bridle, leading us around like dumb animals? I simply can't imagine the Lord sitting in front of the television screen watching several hours of the soaps each day.

Self-discipline is essential to revitalize the self-esteem of those caught in the soap opera web. For the Christian, a new, stronger self-image is based on the realization that we are created in God's image and renewed in the image of Christ. "Therefore if any person is (engrafted) in Christ, the Messiah, he is (a new creature altogether) a new creation; the old (previous moral and spiritual condition) has passed away. Behold, the fresh and new has come."[12] As the new and fresh self-image begins to emerge, His strength leads to more self-discipline; as we increase self-discipline, self-confidence and self-esteem blossom.

Those Sensational Soaps

We "put on the new nature (the regenerate self) created in God's image...."[13]

The Bible says, "Strip yourselves of your former nature — put off and discard your old unrenewed self — which characterized your previous manner of life and becomes corrupt through lusts and desires that spring from delusion; and be constantly renewed in the spirit of your mind — having a fresh mental and spiritual attitude...."[14] It also exhorts..." Do not be conformed to this world — this age, fashioned after and adapted to its external, superficial customs. But be transformed (changed) by the [entire] renewal of your mind — by its new ideals and its new attitudes — so that you may prove [for yourselves] what is the good and acceptable and perfect will of God...."[15] If we are *constantly* renewed in our minds with God's Word and have a fresh mental and spiritual attitude, worry over soap problems will not seem important.

We are constantly putting on this new nature through prayer and meditation which renews the mind and erases anxiety. It is not in God's plan for Christians to worry about *anything* — much less be concerned over the problems and situations of imaginary television characters. We are commanded to ..."not fret or have any anxiety about anything, but in every circumstance and in everything by prayer and petition [definite requests] with thanksgiving continue to make your wants known to God...."[16]

Any Christian can burst the "soap bubble" which has a grip on his life if the following four things are acted upon:

Recognize and acknowledge the addiction.

Begin to replace the habit with positive actions.

Practice self-discipline.

Fellowship with the Lord in prayer and meditation of the Word.

When the addiction is no longer a threat, the psychological problems and needs which caused it can then be dealt with. But healing will only come after self-discipline and self-renewal have transformed the mind, creating a new life-style. Escape from the bondage of Satan's web releases us to become... "children of God without blemish (faultless, unrebukable) in the midst of a crooked and wicked generation — [spiritually] perverted and perverse. Among whom you are seen as bright lights — stars or beacons shining out clearly — in the [dark] world...."[17]

Notes

Chapter 1 Hooked on the Soaps
[1] David P. Phillips, "The Impact of Fictional Television Stories on U.S. Adult Fatalities: New Evidence on the Effect of the Mass Media on Violence" (Department of Sociology, University of California, San Diego, California, 1980), p. 5.
[2] Ibid.
[3] D. E. Tucker, "A Multivariate Analysis of Soap Opera Viewers" (a doctoral dissertation), Bowling Green State University, 1977, in "Impact of Fictional Television Stories," David Phillips, 1980, p. 6.
[4] N. Katzman, "Television Soap Operas: What's Going on Anyway?" *Public Opinion Quarterly* 36 (1972): 200-12.
[5] Robert La Guardia, *The Wonderful World of T.V. Soap Operas* (New York: Random House, 1978), p. 144.
[6] Ibid., p. 145.
[7] Lorraine Smith, "People Are Hungry for Love, Respect and Kindness," *Daytimers Magazine*, Vol. 6, No. 2 (May, 1982): 44-5.
[8] Ibid.
[9] Ibid.

Chapter 2 "Tune in Tomorrow For..."
[1] Elaine Carrington, *Rosemary*, in Madeline Edmondson and David Rounds, *The Soaps* (Briarcliff Manor, New York: Stein and Day Publishers, 1973), p. 52.
[2] Edmondson and Rounds, *The Soaps*, pp. 24-5.
[3] Ibid., p. 25.
[4] Ibid., p. 26.
[5] Ibid.
[6] Ibid., p. 34.
[7] Ibid., p. 38.
[8] Ibid., p. 41.
[9] Ibid., p. 45.
[10] Ibid.

Chapter 3   Soaps Burst Into Big Business
[1] Charlotte-Ann Lucas, "How to Retail a Texas Ranch," *Dallas Times Herald* (Friday, May 28, 1982).

Chapter 4   Husbands, Wives and All Our Children
[1] David P. Phillips, "The Impact of Fictional Television Stories on U.S. Adult Fatalities: New Evidence on the Effect of the Mass Media on Violence" (Department of Sociology, University of California, San Diego, California, 1980), p. 5.
[2] Ibid.
[3] Joan Robbins, "The Impact of Television on Children," *Dawn Magazine* (February, 1982), pp. 4, 5.
[4] N. Katzman, "Television Soap Operas: What's Go-

ing on Anyway?" *Public Opinion Quarterly* 36 (1972): 200-12.

Chapter 5 "Help Me! Dr. Katz"
[1] Agnes Nixon in "Soap-inspired Public-service Idea Deserves Support," Gary Deeb, *Chicago Sun Times*, (February, 1982), p. 41.
[2] Ibid.
[3] Ibid.
[4] Phillip DeMuth and Elizabeth Barton, "Soap Gets in Your Mind," *Psychology Today* (July, 1982), pp. 73-4.
[5] Ibid.
[6] Ibid.
[7] Ibid.
[8] Ibid.
[9] Ibid.
[10] Manuela Soares, *The Soap Opera Book* (New York: Harmony Books, © 1978 by Latham Publishing), p. 21. (Used by permission of Harmony Books).
[11] DeMuth and Barton, "Soaps," pp. 73-4.
[12] Madeline Edmondson and David Rounds, *The Soaps* (Briarcliff Manor, New York: Stein and Day Publishers, 1973), p. 15.
[13] Ibid.
[14] David P. Phillips, Abstract to "The Impact of Fictional Television Stories on U.S. Adult Fatalities: New Evidence on the Effect of the Mass Media on Violence" (Department of Sociology, University of California, San Diego, California, 1980).
[15] Ibid.

Chapter 6 Sensational or Sinsational?
[1] 1 Peter 4:15.
[2] Eph. 5:3-5.
[3] Gal. 5:19, 20, The Living Bible.
[4] Eph. 4:31.
[5] Prov. 15:27.
[6] Prov. 16:18.
[7] Eph. 5:7, 8, 11, 12, 15, 16.
[8] Matt. 7:16-18.
[9] Mark 7:20-23.
[10] 2 Tim. 4:3, 4.

Chapter 7 Bursting the Soap Bubble
[1] 1 Cor. 10:12.
[2] Isa. 59:4-6.
[3] 2 Tim. 2:16, 17; 3:6, 7.
[4] Phil. 4:8, 9.
[5] Col. 3:2.
[6] 1 Thess. 5:21, 22.
[7] Isa. 40:31 paraphrased.
[8] Phil. 4:13.
[9] 2 Cor. 13:3.
[10] Eph. 4:14.
[11] Psa. 32:9.
[12] 2 Cor. 5:17.
[13] Eph. 4:24.
[14] Eph. 4:22, 23.
[15] Rom. 12:2.
[16] Phil. 4:6.
[17] Phil. 2:15.

All correspondence
to the author may be
addressed to:

Aloha & Company
P.O. Box 1181
Cameron, TX 76520

Another Book by Velma Angel
The Practical Woman

If you are a woman who is truly concerned about the ever-increasing divorce rate, the growing number of broken homes, and the insidious, continual disintegration of the concept of the family as the cornerstone of a free and healthy society, you'll want to read this vital, inspirational book.

**Topics Include
How to Handle:**

- Attitudes
- Fears
- Insecurities
- Complaining
- Marriage
- Sex

Plus

- Beauty Hints
- Recipes
- Menus
- Meal Planning

and Much More!

Retail $9.95

What the Reviewers Are Saying

"Outstanding" — "I can say it is one of the best books I have ever read. The information that it gives and the quality of the book is very outstanding."
— **Tammy Faye Bakker**
PTL Club

"Excellent" — "Velma Angel shares the practical aspects of being a woman, appearance, attitudes, relationship and care of the home. An excellent source, particularly for teaching young women."
— **Virtue Magazine**

ORDER FORM

Aloha & Company
P.O. Box 1181
Cameron, TX 76520

PRINT PLAINLY SO WE CAN PROPERLY READ YOUR NAME

NAME_____ DATE_____

ADDRESS _____ *STREET ADDRESS NECESSARY FOR UPS DELIVERY* □ *DO NOT SEND UPS*

CITY_____ STATE_____ ZIP_____

QUANTITY	DESCRIPTION	UNIT PRICE	TOTAL
	THE PRACTICAL WOMAN	$9.95	
	THE PRACTICAL WOMAN, Teachers Manual	$8.95	
		TOTAL ORDER	
	Packing and Shipping Chart *PLEASE USE THIS CHART TO COMPLETE YOUR PACKING/SHIPPING COST:* **Orders** 1 Book................add $1.00 for each additional book add 50¢ per book	PACKAGING & SHIPPING	
CHARGE YOUR PURCHASE Check One: □ VISA □ MASTER CARD [ ][ ][ ][ ] EXP. DATE MO. YEAR INTERBANK NO [ ][ ][ ][ ] X ......*Sign your name as it appears on your Bank Card*		TOTAL AMOUNT ENCLOSED	